THE ROYAL AIR FORCE BENEVOLENT FUND'S

INTERNATIONAL AIR TATTOO 94

RAF FAIRFORD 30-31 JULY

THE BEST IN
MILITARY AVIATION

Peter R March

THE ROYAL AIR FORCE BENEVOLENT FUND

ISBN 0 9516581 7 4

INTERNATIONAL AIR TATTOO 94

CONTENTS

Published by

The Royal Air Force Benevolent Fund Enterprises Publications Unit, Building 15, RAF Fairford, Glos GL7 4DL, England

Publishing Director: **Paul A. Bowen**
Publishing Manager: **Claire Lock**

Compiled & Edited by **Peter R. March**
Research: **Ben Dunnell & Brian Strickland**
Editorial Assistant: **Daniel March**
Additional Material: **Robby Robinson**

Photography by the International Air Tattoo 94 Photo Services Team:
Gordon Bartley (GB), John Dunnell (JD), Graham Finch (GF), Andrew March (APM), Daniel March (DJM) & Brian Strickland (BSS)
Photo Manager: **Peter R. March (PRM)**

Cover artwork: **Wilfred Hardy** GAvA
Design: **Graham Finch Design**
Typeset: **Jean Strickland**

Paper courtesy of Interfor Limited
Printed in Hong Kong

ISBN 0 9516581 7 4

Four Hercules variants formed the centrepiece of the Hercules 40th anniversary line-up – an AC-130A gunship, a ski-equipped LC-130H and the 2,000th aircraft off the production line (a C-130H) from the USAF, plus *Snoopy* – a W2 used by the RAF for meteorological research. PRM

INTERNATIONAL AIR TATTOO 94

THE BEST IN MILITARY AVIATION

The 1994 International Air Tattoo held at RAF Fairford on 30-31 July presented the very best in military aviation, at what was again the biggest event of its kind in the world this year. With over 300 aircraft taking part, including more than 40 C-130 Hercules, there was plenty to see, both on the ground and in the air, to please the large number of people that attended. The spectators had to put up with some unsettled weather, with rain early on Saturday followed by sunshine and a longer downpour on the second day, but they remained undaunted. For the many enthusiasts who watched the aircraft arrivals in the days before and the departures on the Monday after the show, the weather was much kinder.

There were several themes for IAT 94 – the 40th anniversary of the Lockheed C-130 Hercules, the 25th anniversary of the first flight of Concorde and its testing days at Fairford, the 50th birthday of RAF Fairford itself and the Royal Air Force Benevolent Fund's 75th Anniversary. But it was the sheer number of Hercules in the static display and in the flying programme that will be the principal memory of this the 15th Air Tattoo since the first of these major

international events was held at North Weald, Essex in 1971. Two Air Tattoos were held at this former Battle of Britain airfield (1971-72) before it moved to RAF Greenham Common. The airshows grew rapidly to fill this huge, largely unused USAF base, with International Air Tattoos staged in 1973, 1974, 1976, 1977, 1979, 1981 and 1983. A new home was required following the Cruise missile deployment and the actions of the so-called 'peace women' and the airshow took place at RAF Fairford for the first time in 1985. This was followed by IATs in 1987, 1989, 1991, 1993 and again this year, 1994.

Many of those past Tattoos have featured large numbers of *Fat Alberts*, especially the 1979 C-130 25th anniversary and the 1987 Skylift meets, but this year saw special efforts to create a 40-strong static line. Operational commitments, particularly the international relief effort in Rwanda and US preparations for military intervention in Haiti, saw several Hercules lost from the line, notably the Royal Netherlands AF's new C-130H-30, plus the French, Norwegian and Southern Air Transport aircraft. The entire Turkish AF

3

contingent including its C-130 support for the F-5s, F-104s and F-4s could not attend due to financial constraints. At the end of the day it was RAF Lyneham, home for the RAF's fleet of Hercules, that brought the total to within four of the 'one for each of the C-130's years', and with the contribution of half-a-dozen or so in the flying programme to over 40. But even Lyneham's contribution had to be scaled down on the second day as more aircraft were required to go on standby for flights to Africa.

At the forefront of the line-up was *First Lady*, the USAF's AC-130A (53-3129) that was first off the production line in 1954 and is today operated by the 711th Special Operations Squadron of the USAF Reserve. At the other end of the production scale there was the 2000th aircraft, the immaculate C-130H (91-1231) provided by the 165th Airlift Squadron of the Kentucky Air National Guard. The USAF also brought the ski-equipped LC-130H from the 139th Airlift Squadron, New York Air National Guard that was awarded the *Concours d'Elegance* for the best turned out Hercules at the event. The only real newcomer to the Hercules line-up at Fairford was the Royal Malaysian Air Force with its stretched C-130H-30. Other highlights included the appearances of a Brazilian AF C-130E, Royal Air Force of Oman C-130H and one of only two stretched US Marine Corps KC-130T-30s so far delivered, coming from VMGR-452. The appearance of the DRA Met Research Flight's unique Hercules W2 *Snoopy* was also very welcome, particularly as its future remains uncertain. In the flying display the tactical demonstration by two RAF C1s was impressive with a double vehicle and troop off-load. Five more Lyneham-based examples flew by in close company, while a Swedish AF C-130E (the first to be delivered to a European air force) gave its usual solo display.

It was certainly not just the Hercules that caught the attention at IAT 94. The East European air arms – from the Czech and Slovak Republics and Russia – made impressive contributions to the static and flying displays. Russian Naval Aviation had its first involvement in a UK display, with a Tu-142M *Bear-F* flown in by the Training Regiment from Pskov. For the flying programme Russian Air Force Long-Range Strategic Aviation provided a Tu-95MS *Bear-H* from the 182nd Heavy Bomber Squadron at Mozdok. Unfortunately, for technical reasons it was unable to display on the Saturday but did make a majestic flypast on Sunday. The Czech Air Force had a Mil Mi-17 helicopter in the static display and a specially-marked MiG-21MF, while the Slovak Air Force had a grey tiger-striped MiG-29UB alongside. The Slovaks also sent a MiG-21MF that was presented to the RAF Benevolent Fund to be auctioned at a future date to raise money for the Fund. It was received from the Slovak Defence Minister by Prince Michael of Kent at a brief ceremony on Saturday. In the flying display the Czech AF's solo MiG-21MF *Fishbed*, Su-25K *Frogfoot*, L-39MS *Albatros* and Su-22M4 *Fitter* were augmented by the *Szobi Kvartet* of L-410UVP Turbolets all giving their excellent displays. But the highlight

The Hercules Tactical Demonstration was just one of IAT 94's highlights. PRM

4

A pair of Czech Air Force Mi-24 *Hinds* gave an exciting flying display. BSS

was undoubtedly the Prostejov-based duo of Mi-24D *Hinds*. This team, displaying in Britain for the first time was to many spectators the star of the flying, firing flares as part of an excellent sequence. Not to be outdone the Slovak AF also displayed a solo *Fishbed*, a MiG-29 and the six L-39Cs of the *White Albatros* team. An appreciable and very welcome contribution.

Other highlights of the static display included the first UK airshow appearance by a French AF Mirage IVP, flown in from EB1/91 at Mont-de-Marsan. This was one aircraft whose appearance at IAT had long been awaited. More of the same generation of front-line aircraft came with two pairs of Italian AF F-104S and TF-104G Starfighters, all in the green/grey camouflage scheme. The Swedish AF sent a J-32E Lansen of F16M which was accompanied by a J-35 Draken from F10, the latter in grey with large dayglo codes on its upper wing

IAT94 saw the first appearance at a UK airshow by a French Air Force Mirage IVP. DJM

Two Russian *Bears* attended IAT94. This example, a Russian Naval Aviation Tu-142M *Bear-F*, was displayed in the static park. PRM

surfaces. The Lansen was another first-timer at IAT.

There were more uncommon aircraft types on show. The Finnish Air Force participated for the first time with Redigo from the Flight Test Centre where it is undergoing pre-service trials. The Spanish Navy brought a pair of Matadors – no not the bull-fighters but Spanish Navy Harriers. The AV-8S (Harrier 1) was for the flying display and the TAV-8S (Harrier T4) for static display, along with a supporting Citation II. An OH-6A Cayuse from the Rhode Island Army National Guard had a novel transatlantic lift inside the RI ANG's C-130E that came for the Hercules Meet.

Nine hours of flying on both days took in plenty from overseas air arms alongside the items already mentioned. The Swedish AF Hercules was joined by a J-35 Draken from F10, while the Italian AF RSV test pilots created a big impression with the Aeritalia G222 and a new P180 Avanti mini-airliner displays. The latter's routine included a tailslide-cum-pushover as well as near inverted manoeuvres. There were fewer aerobatic teams this year but the regulars such as the *Patrouille de France*, Spanish AF *Aguila*, the ever impressive *Frecce Tricolori*, the *Royal Jordanian Falcons*, the RAF *Red Arrows* and, for the last time, the six Hunter F58s of the *Patrouille Suisse* made their mark. It was announced that the latter team will fly F-5E Tiger IIs next year after the retirement of the Hunters.

Vintage transports, apart from the Hercules, had a prominent part in the flying display. What was billed as 'the first and the last' flying displays by the A&AEE's Comet 4C was very well received by the crowd. There was better news

of the Comet after the event, as it seems likely that it will now continue in use at Boscombe Down for up to four more years. Although the British Airways' Concorde G-BOAC was not actually participating in the flying programme, its arrival and departure on charter flights was a popular way to remind spectators that the supersonic airliner has been flying for 25 years and that the British flight test centre was at Fairford.

Other historic aircraft marked the 50th anniversary of D-Day – the Battle of Britain Memorial Flight with its Lancaster, Spitfire V and Hurricane, and the Dutch Spitfire Flight's Mk IX Spitfire MK732. The latter was one of the aircraft that shot down the first Luftwaffe aircraft over the D-Day beaches on 6 June 1944. The Royal Jordanian Air Force Historic Flight made its public début but sadly with only one of its two vintage jets (the Vampire T55) on the public days. The Flight's Hunter T53 was only seen during its evening rehearsal on the Thursday prior to the show. While being refuelled at Bournemouth one of its wing tanks was ruptured, preventing it from flying in to Fairford for the weekend display. This was particularly disappointing for the Flight as King Hussein was present on Sunday hoping to see the Hunter and Vampire in action for the first time.

The weekend was rounded off on Sunday night with the prizegiving, four flying display trophies being awarded. Flying Officer Mark Discombe was the recipient of the *UK Display Trophy* for his No 1 FTS Tucano display, while the *Superkings Solo Jet Aerobatic Trophy* was presented to Capt Ingemar Axelsson, pilot of the Swedish AF Draken. Winner of the B&Q *International Display Sword* for the best display by an

The world's last flying DH Comet, operated by the A&AEE at Boscombe Down, gave its first flying display at IAT94. PRM

The *Patrouille Suisse* performed for the last time at an IAT display with their familiar Hunters, due to be replaced with F-5E Tiger IIs in 1995.

overseas performer was Capt Pierre Pougheon, who provided a dynamic performance in the French AF Mirage 2000B. This was the third Fairford event in succession at which one of the flying awards has gone to a Mirage 2000 display. Finally, the *Patrouille Suisse*, led by Major Frans Ramseier received the *Sir Douglas Bader Trophy*, presented by Shell UK Oil for the best overall flying demonstration.

Once again, the organisers presented a wide range of aeroplanes to a large and appreciative audience. Despite attempts by the weather to put a dampner on the proceedings IAT 94 achieved its prime objectives – to entertain and to raise much-needed income for the RAF Benevolent Fund. The efforts of the huge number of IAT volunteers involved in presenting the event was rewarded after the event when the Controller of the Royal Air Force Benevolent Fund, Air Chief Marshal Sir Roger Palin announced that it was a safe, enjoyable, entertaining and profitable air tattoo.

Colourful line-up of the CASA Aviojets flown by the *Patrulla Aguila*. APM

Welcome visitors to IAT 94 were the Spanish Navy, who provided two Matadors – a two seat TAV-8S and single seat AV-8S (below). APM

The three Boeing Stearman biplanes of the *Cadburys Crunchie Flying Circus* gave their now traditional IAT opening flying display on both days. Based at Rendcomb, just north of Cirencester, Gloucestershire, they are the only professional wing-walking team in Europe. The Stearman pilots were Vic Norman, Mike Dentith and Matthew Hall, with wingwalkers Mandy Pantall, Gemma Lewis and Sara Cubitt, respectively. DJM

Shorts Tucano T1 ZF408, wearing the white rose of Yorkshire emblem on its fuselage together with the crossed swords 75th anniversary emblem of No 1 FTS on its tail, was flown by Flying Officer Mark Discombe. His outstanding display brought him the UK Display Sword, presented by the IAT Team in memory of the late Air Chief Marshal Sir Alasdair Steadman, for the best flying demonstration by a UK participant at IAT 94. PRM

This recently up-graded Westland Lynx SH-14D of the Royal Netherlands Navy gave a search and rescue demonstration. Based at Naval Air Station De Kooy it is one of 22 Lynx jointly operated by No 7 Squadron in the training, transport and SAR role and by No 860 Squadron on board frigates for ASW and ASUW duties. Prior to coming to Fairford this helicopter had been involved in operations in the Adriatic. DJM

Equipped with six L-39C Albatroses the *White Albatros* aerobatic team of the Slovak Air Force, appeared at IAT for the second year. Led again by Lt Col Ivan Chvojka the six pilots are instructors at the Aeronautical Academy 5th Training Wing, No 1 Squadron at Kosice in east Slovakia. New for this year are the L-39's extended fuel tanks and improved coloured smoke generators. IAT 94 at Fairford was one of seven displays undertaken this year by the team outside of Slovakia. GF

Unfortunately the German AF Tornado ECR (46-34) was unable to display on either of the weekend days owing to the bad weather at its allotted time. It did manage a high-speed taxi and performed a full practice display prior to the event. This latest version of the Tornado IDS is equipped with FLIR (forward looking infrared), with HUD (head-up display), ODIN (operational data link) and carries the HARM (high-speed anti-radar missile). Based with No 1 Squadron, Fighter Bomber Wing 32 at Lechfeld, the Tornado was to have been displayed by Capt Michael Verweinen. PRM

The BAe Harrier has recently notched up its 25th anniversary in Royal Air Force service. Now in his second display season, the Harrier GR7 display pilot, Flight Lieutenant Rob Lee is an instructor on No 20(Reserve) Squadron (the Harrier OCU) at RAF Wittering. The OCU trains Harrier pilots and also runs courses for Harrier Instrument Rating Examiners, Qualified Weapons Instructors and Electronic Warfare Instructors. APM

The Alenia G222 medium and short range transport aircraft is a regular performer at IAT, where it demonstrates its short field and slow-flying capabilities, steep turns and aileron rolls. The aircraft (RS-51) comes from the Italian Flight Test Centre – Reparto Sperimentale Volo (RSV) – No 311 Squadron at Pratica di Mare, near Rome. This year the G222 was flown by Major Fabio Consoli, a former operational test pilot on the F-104 Starfighter. The propeller tip vortices reflect the damp conditions when the G222 performed. GF

The Czech Air Force Sukhoi Su-22M-4 *Fitter* was flown by Col Frantisek Cisar, a 42 year old pilot from 32 ZTL at Námest nad Oslavou – who has been display flying the Su-22M-4 since 1989. The *Fitter* is in operational service with most East European Air Forces, as well as other countries that have received support from the former Soviet Union. The aircraft is unusual that it is a variable geometry aircraft that was developed from a fixed wing version – the original Su-7 *Fitter* – A having first flown in the mid-1950s. PRM

The Tornado GR1 display aircraft came from No 15 (Reserve) Squadron – the Tactical Weapons Conversion Unit based at RAF Lossiemouth. The 1994 airshow aircraft (ZA559) is specially painted in a maritime grey scheme, with 'XV' on the fin. As such it was the RAF's first all grey Tornado, that has since been followed by the GR1Bs that newly equip Nos 12 and 617 Squadrons at the Scottish airfield. The display pilot was Flight Lieutenant Mark Roberts with Flight Lieutenant Dave Morris as navigator. Both are instructors on the TWCU. PRM

The *Szobi Kvartet* is a unique team of Czech Air Force Let 410 UVPs, which made its UK début at IAT 93. The quartet was led this year by Major Vladimír Randa in Szobi 1. The team was first formed in 1989 by Lt Col Josef Szobi, who retired from flying three years ago, but has since remained as team manager. It is currently based at the lst Squadron, 36th Composite Aviation Transport Regiment at Pardubice, having originally been with the 1st Composite Aviation Transport Regiment at Mosnov. This season the team is sponsored by the Iron Works of Trinec. GF

The *Patrulla Aguila* is in its tenth season as the Spanish Air Force Aerial Demonstration Team. It has performed at every IAT event since it was formed. The team 'Aguila' (Eagle) is based at the Air Force Academy, at San Javier AB Air Base in Murcia. An important era in its brief history was the 1992 season, when the CASA 101 Aviojet turbofan powered jet trainers received a striking new colour scheme and got coloured-smoke generators. The pilots, previously flying front-line fighter dircraft, are now full-time instructors at the Academy. The leader of the 1994 team is Captain Neito, aged 30, with 2,500 hours flying experience. APM

The Slovak Air Force MiG-21 was flown by Lt Col Frantisek Zsoldos, from the 2nd Squadron of the 1st Fighter Wing, based at Sliac. A graduate from the Czech and Slovak Air Force Academy as a fighter pilot he has experience on the MiG-21, MiG-23 and MiG-29. The MiG-21 *Fishbed* was designed as a lightweight 'air superiority' fighter after the Korean War and first flew on 16 June 1955. PRM

Flight Lieutenant Dave 'Stobes' Stobie, a Qualified Flying and Weapons Instructor and OC Standards Flight at No 7 FTS, RAF Chivenor displayed the royal blue painted HS Hawk T1. The display aircraft is from No 92 (Reserve) Squadron and the paint scheme follows in the tradition started by the No 92 Squadron *Blue Diamonds* display team flying Hunters in the late 1950s. This colour scheme was carried on by the Phantom FGR2s of Nos 19 and 92 Squadrons to mark the disbandment of both squadrons at RAF Wildenrath in 1991. This was the last year that a Chivenor Hawk will display at IAT as the station was set for closure in October 1994. PRM

Below: The Army Air Corps' *Blue Eagles* helicopter display team are second only to the *Red Arrows* as the longest running team in the country, having been formed in 1968 from instructors at Middle Wallop. The 1994 display saw an opening manoeuvre that had the four Gazelles forming an inclined diamond formation, which was just large enough to fly the solo Lynx AH7 through. Pulling up into a backflip, that has become the trademark of the *Blue Eagles'* Lynx, the team continued its coordinated and original routine. GF

MAD GER STYRKA

Another first time appearance at IAT was a display by a Saab J35-J Draken from the Swedish Air Force 3 Fighter Squadron, F10 Wing at Angelholm, near Malmo. The pilot was Captain Ingemar Axelsson aged 36, who has been a display pilot since 1991. For his excellent programme 'Axel' was awarded the Superkings Trophy, presented by Imperial Tobacco for the overall best solo jet demonstration. The first flight of the Draken was way back on 25 October 1955, but it remains active in Sweden, Austria and Finland. The display aircraft was the J35-J version with upgraded radar and weapons system. PRM/GF

The distinctive shape of a twin-engine pusher five-bladed propeller, with three lifting surfaces, made a novel addition to the IAT flying display. Newly delivered to the Italian Air Force, the Piaggio P180 Avanti was displayed by Major Massimo Baroco from the Italian Flight Test Centre (RSV) at Pratica di Mare. The white-painted Avanti is a nine-seat transport aircraft with an astonishing aerobatic capability which was shown to full advantage by the display pilot. PRM

The Swedish Air Force display Hercules has been seen at IAT on previous occasions and is renowned for a spirited display sequence. Sweden has two C-130E Hercules (E-1 versions with A-15 engines) based at the Air Transport Wing F7 at Satenäs, of which 84001 (841) was the display aircraft. Finished in a high gloss olive brown paint scheme, with prominent yellow lettering, the Swedish Hercules' always stand out from its contemporaries. During its low banking passes, with the rear loading ramp lowered, a crew-member in white overalls waved to the crowd. GB

Right: **They still retain the 'Shark' emblem on the rear empennage, although the two Royal Navy Helicopter Display Team Gazelle HT2s from 705 Naval Air Squadron at RNAS Culdrose are sadly no longer part of that famous team. The pilots of the surviving display duo, Lieutenants Mark Fulford and Scott Booker are both Qualified Helicopter Instructors who practise and attend displays outside the normal working hours of the squadron.** APM

Although the colourful Czech Air Force Sukhoi Su-25K *Frogfoot* 9013 with the frog emblem on its tail was present again at IAT this year, it was parked in the static aircraft display. The camouflaged *Frogfoot* 1002, with a distinctive red, white and blue fin together with a shark's mouth nose, was the display aircraft for 1994. The display pilot was Major Leos Liska, aged 33, from the 30th Combat Regiment at Pardubice in the Czech Republic. This year the 30th celebrated its 50th anniversary. PRM

FLYING DISPLAY

Nimrod MR2 XV246, flown in the second day's display was a replacement aircraft brought in on the Sunday morning from RAF Kinloss to replace XV239 that was unable to fly on the Saturday after a contretemps with a runway sweeper lorry whilst taxiing. The No 201 Squadron crew gave a lively display to celebrate the Nimrod's Silver Anniversary year. PRM

The German Navy Tornado (46+14) from MFG2 (2 Squadron of Naval Air Wing 2), based at Eggebek, came off somewhat better with the weather than its GAF counterpart. This version of the Tornado is used in the anti-shipping role, fitted with four Kormoran or four Harm anti-ship missiles. The display pilot was Lieutenant Commander 'Dappi' Dappert and the navigator Lieutenant Jurgen Thomsen. APM/PRM

Lt Col Eugenio Lupinacci, the third pilot from No 311 Squadron, Reparto Sperimentale Volo at Pratica di Mare to take part in IAT 94, displayed the Italian Air Force AMX Centaur (MM7131/RS-13). Col Lupinacci is a former operational pilot on F-104 Starfighters and was a 1990 graduate of the Empire Test Pilots School at Boscombe Down. in 1990. He has flown more than 35 different types of aircraft. PRM

Yellow Sea King HAR3 (XZ588) in No 202 Squadron markings, but from the Sea King Training Unit (SKTU) at RAF St Mawgan, made a fleeting visit on Saturday to give its display, but did not land at Fairford. It was flown by Flight Lieutenants Steve Martin and Bob Sommerville, both instructors at the SKTU. The unit's task is to train all aircrew who join the Search and Rescue units that operate Sea King HAR3s. GF

Now in its 21st display season, the Royal Netherlands Air Force helicopter display team performed its usual precision sequence, including the famous carousel. Flying its customary four Alouette III helicopters, in their red, white and blue colour schemes, the 1994 team was led by Capt Peter Hardenbol, aged 33, in his second season with the *Grasshoppers*. The team is part of No 300 Squadron at Deelen Air Base near to Arnhem. APM

It was a nostalgic occasion at IAT for those who particularly wanted to see the rare display of a DH106 Comet. Comet C4C XS235 *Canopus* first flew on 26 September 1963 from Chester to Hatfield. The aircraft was specially modified for A&AEE Boscombe Down as a flying laboratory to test navigation and radio equipment. It was delivered to Boscombe Down on 2 December 1963 and has totalled only 8,000 flying hours over the last 30 years. XS235 is the last flying example of the world's first four-jet passenger aircraft. An impressive display was performed by Boscombe test pilot Flt Lt Mark Seymour – an ex-Nimrod display pilot and graduate of ETPS. On the Sunday it made a spectacular landing after a heavy storm on the very wet runway, almost disappearing from view under a mass of spray! APM/PRM/GF

The Gloucestershire Ambulance Service MBB Bo105DBS/4 G-BUXS, on loan from Bond Helicopters, took time off from its emergency services stand-by to provide an aerial platform for the customary IAT photo-run on the first day of the show. The air-to-ground photographs included in this book were taken by the editor, here caught at the other end of the camera lens. APM

The shiny, bare metal finish of the Czech MiG-21MF 4307 was in marked contrast to the special markings on its compatriot in the static aircraft park. The IAT display was performed by veteran military test pilot Colonel Frantisek Hlavnicka, more usually known as Frankie. He has flown 26 versions of ten aircraft types and has been a display pilot since 1983 as a member of the Delta F Aerobatic Group, of the Czech Air Force, with the 1st Sqn at the Test Pilots Aviation Centre at Cáslav Air Base. The Delta F team dates back to 1957 when it was originally formed with MiG-15s. GF

Another Czech Air Force participant in the flying display was up-dated Aero L-39MS Albatros, flown by 54 year old test pilot Lt Col Victor Nohel. The aircraft is based at the Czech AF Research Institute at Prague/Kbely. Known as the L-39MS, it is also called the L-59 in its export form for overseas customers. This was the second year that 0004, the fourth production aircraft has been at IAT. The L-39MS has a more powerful engine, modified cockpit canopy, new avionics, weapons system, HUD and bigger wing-tip tanks. PRM

The Aeronautica Militare Italiana *Frecce Tricolori* can trace its history back to the Campoformido aerobatic school of 1930. The present national aerobatic display team dates from 1 July 1951 when the 313th Aerobatic Training Squadron was established at Rivolto del Fruili flying F-86 Sabres. Subsequently flying Fiat G-91s and since 1982 the Aermacchi MB339A/PAN, the *Frecce* still flies a formation of nine aircraft, plus a soloist, and is therefore, the largest military formation team in the world. Like its RAF counterparts, the *Frecce's* pilots are able to quickly become combat-ready and the aircraft converted to armed configuration for duty as an offensive support squadron. To date the team has given more than 1,700 public performances. It has been led since 1992 by Gianluigi Zanovello, aged 38, Commandante del 313° Gruppo Addestramento Acrobatico. GF

Always a colourful performer at IAT, the Royal Netherlands Air Force solo F-16A (J251) was no exception this year. The display aircraft had a modified red, white and blue colour scheme on the upper surfaces and new tail markings that included a tiger emblem on the tail. The 1994 display pilot was 32 year old Capt Peter 'Fingers' Janssen, who is normally a test pilot at Volkel Air Base and as an instructor pilot at No 313 Squadron at Twenthe. As usual the wing-tip 'smokewinders' were used to maximum effect, particularly in the 'high-alpha' configuration fly-past. DIM

Saturday's *Albert* formation of five Hercules came from RAF Lyneham. Leading the flight was Squadron Leader Stu Vince from No 57(R) Squadron in a Hercules C1. Trailing its flight refuelling hose, a Hercules C1K was flown by Flt Lt Nick Young from No 24 Squadron on the first day, but was missing on Sunday when the formation was reduced to four. Also in the formation was – Hercules C3 flown by Sqn Ldr Chris Bartle of No 70 Sqn; another C3 captained by Flt Lt Mark Touzel, of No 47 Sqn and bringing up the rear Sqn Ldr Laurie Ramage of No 30 Sqn flying a C1. GF

Flying displays of the Mil Mi-24 *Hind D* helicopter have been performed almost since its introduction into service with the Czech Air Force in 1978. However, this was their first display appearance in the UK and gave arguably one of the best helicopter displays to be seen at Fairford. The two machines – 4011, in a white colour scheme that incorporated a 'tiger' rear fuselage, contrasted with the 'shark-mouth' marking and standard camouflage on 0216. The leading pilot was Lt Col Jiri Rohacek, aged 54, with Major Jiri Valach, aged 39, as number two. The *Hinds* are based at the 51st Helo Regt at Prostejov. GF/APM/PRM/BSS

The *Royal Jordanian Falcons* team, which was formed in 1976, represent the Hashemite Kingdom of Jordan. In their second year with the Extra 300, the team has made regular visits to IAT. The *Falcons* is a specialised department of the Royal Jordanian airline and operates from the team's headquarters at the Amman-Marka International airport. It operates on a full-time basis and the pilots are specially selected from the Jordanian Air Force and the national airline. The *Falcons* team is led by Major Majed Al-Kayed, with Capt Nart Alkhas on the left wing and Capt Omar Howaij on the right wing. No 4/Solo is Capt Omar Belal. DJM

The all-black Jaguar GR1A XX116, with the 'Saint' emblem on its tail, gave its usual spirited display with a banked turn immediately after take-off. The Jaguar was flown by Flt Lt Andy Cubin, a Qualified Flying Instructor from No 16 (Reserve) Squadron at RAF Lossiemouth. The squadron is the Operational Conversion Unit for the Jaguar and its role is to train pilots for frontline squadrons based at RAF Coltishall. GF/APM

The *Patrouille de France* celebrated its fortieth anniversary in October 1993, hence the tails of its Alpha Jets carry the number '40' this year. The *Patrouille*, a French Air Force Unit, is attached to the Air Force Academy at Salon de Provence. The leader in 1994 was Major Phillippe Connan, aged 36, who is in his third year. His deputy, Major William Kurtz, aged 33, will be taking over for 1995. The pilots train from November to April totalling 160 flights, at a rate of two flights per day. They are all volunteers and are with the team for an average period of three years, coming from combat squadrons. GF

The Belgian F-16A Fighting Falcon (FA-107) from the 1st Squadron of the 2nd Wing at Florennes, was piloted by Cdt Jean-Jacques de Wael, who has been flying the F-16 since 1989. The ten minute display by the Belgian F-16 showed the manoeuvrability of this fighter, keeping within the confines of the airfield boundary for most of the performance. APM

The Hercules Tactical Demonstration at IAT 94 this year was a two-ship display. Captain of the lead aircraft was Sqn Ldr Nigel Watson from No 57 (Reserve) Squadron at RAF Lyneham and the second C-130 was in the hands of Sqn Ldr Don Macintosh, from the Standards and Evaluation Unit at Lyneham. The two aircraft approached line astern, breaking downwind for a low level circuit at slightly different heights. The two aircraft then demonstrated TALO (Tactical Air Landing Operations), aiming to touch down together – an operation which would normally be carried out at night. This technique allows up to 80 fully armed troops to be off-loaded as close as possible to their objective. At Fairford, a Scimitar and Land Rover, together with troops, off-loaded from each aircraft. Once the troops were out of the C-130s the aircraft backed down the runway for a tactical take-off. GF/APM

This year only one MiG-29 took part in the IAT flying display. This was MiG-29A *Fulcrum* 9308 of the Slovak Air Force, finished in standard camouflage, and based with 1 SLP/1 Letka at Sliac in the Slovak Republic. The display pilot was Lt Col Jozef Dunaj, aged 40, who previously flew MiG-29s at Zatec. APM

The heavy formation from nearby RAF Brize Norton performed a single flypast, with refuelling drogues deployed. Tristar KC1 ZD950 was flown by Sqn Ldr Phil Carr of No 216 Squadron, VC10 C1K XV109 by Flt Lt Roy Wheatley of No 10 Squadron and VC10 K3 ZA149 by Flt Lt Simon Wall of No 101 Sqn. The Tristar KC1 is a strategic tanker/freighter/passenger aircraft with extra fuel and two refuelling hose drum units under the rear fuselage. The VC10 C1K has a joint air transport/air refuelling role and has two refuelling pods, whereas the VC10 K3 (an ex-Super VC10) is a three point tanker. This K3 (ZA149) is the first of the type to be repainted in the new blue-grey overall scheme. DJM

A newcomer to the air show scene was the *Royal Jordanian Historic Flight* with its Vampire T55 (G-BVLM). Vampires were the first jet aircraft to be flown by the Royal Jordanian AF, the RAF having donated three T11s like this one, and ten FB9s to the new air force. This actual aircraft was built in 1958 as a T55 for the Swiss Air Force (U-1216). It remained in service until 1989, when it was presented to the RAF Benevolent Fund, in the hope that the RAF would keep it flying. It was purchased by the *Royal Jordanian Historic Flight* and is finished in the colours of No 1 Sqn RJAF. Following refurbishment by Jet Heritage at Bournemouth it first flew for the RJHF on 8 July 1994. Its new companion, the Hunter T7 (G-BOOM), purchased on behalf of the *RJAF Historic Flight* in February 1994, was also scheduled to display at IAT with the Vampire. After it made a brief practice appearance on the Thursday, it became unserviceable at Bournemouth, whilst being prepared to return to Fairford and was unable to leave its base. GF/JD

Right: **Fifty years ago this Spitfire LFIX became one of four to share the honour of making one of the first airborne kills of the D-Day invasion. At the time it was on the strength of No 485 Sqn of the RNZAF. Post-war it was sold by the RAF to the Royal Netherlands Air Force but, by devious routes, MK732 was returned to the UK – where it was used as a source of spare parts for the BBMF. Restoration began in 1990 simultaneously in the UK and Holland. It is now operated by the Dutch Spitfire Group – although based in Holland it is operated on the British civil register as G-HVDM. It made its post-restoration flight on 10 June 1993 and for the 1994 display season it was painted in the former No 485 Squadron D-Day markings.** APM

The Spanish Navy AV-8S Matador made an unfortunate arrival at Fairford, bursting its tyres on landing. With the help of RNAS Yeovilton spares were obtained, and fitted to enable the Harrier to make its display début on the Sunday. It was displayed by Lieut Pedro Galiana of the Spanish Navy's 8th Squadron based at Rota in southern Spain. The 8th Sqn is the only (and last) unit in the world still flying the AV-8S, which is basically the original Harrier GR1/US Marine Corps AV-8A. APM

The *Patrouille Suisse* made its début, with Hawker Hunters F58s, at IAT 79, RAF Greenham Common and won the Shell UK Oil Trophy for the 'best overall display'. The team made its final appearance at IAT 94 with Hunters and won the Sir Douglas Bader Trophy again presented by Shell UK Oil for the 'best flying demonstration'. The Hunters are being withdrawn from service and for 1995 the *Patrouille* will re-equip with Northrop F-5E Tiger IIs. This was the 30th anniversary year of the *Patrouille Suisse* and the Hunter F58s featured a large figure 30 on the tail and the words '30 Jahra Patrouille Suisse' on the rear fuselage. The team leader for 1994 was Major Frans Ramseier. GF/PRM

The F-4 Phantom is a popular performer at IAT, the Luftwaffe providing this year's example, an F-4F Phantom II of JbG-35 based at Pferdsfeld, Germany. JbG-35 has (since early 1994) become a fighter interceptor squadron having previously also been a tactical fighter squadron. The pilot was Major Norbert Lubosch, aged 40 and the navigator was Capt Mike Nauth, aged 33. Currently the F-4F is undergoing an update programme and will fly operationally in the German Air Force for some years to come. APM

In 1993 IAT had the first visit of a Russian Tu-95 *Bear*, albeit not in the public flying display. This year two *Bears* came to Fairford, with one of them – the Russian Air Force Tu-95MS *Bear-H* 34379/23 – participating in the flying on the Sunday. This aircraft came from the Long-Range Strategic Aviation (LRSA) base at Mozdok in Southern Russia. The LRSA has 84 Tu-95 MS bombers operational (19 are at the Uzin AB in the Ukraine). The Tu-95MS was the final production model, equipped for carrying six RKV-15V cruise missiles on a rotary launcher in the weapons bay plus two more on its wingroot pylons. A Tornado F3 of No 25 Squadron escorted the *Bear* into Fairford. APM/BSS

The French Air Force Mirage 2000B again gave an excellent display at IAT, and for the third successive year won a top award. This year Captain Pierre Pougheon, aged 28, based with E Squadron 2/2 'Cote d'Or' at Dijon, won the International Display Sword presented by B&Q for the best flying demonstration by an overseas participant. This was an instance where a reserve/support aircraft can be invaluable. On the Saturday 521/2-FX was the display aircraft and should have also performed on the Sunday, but at the last minute the aircraft went unserviceable and the pilot had to quickly take over 516/2-FM for the display. This was the 'Pierro's' first year as Mirage 2000 display pilot. He is an instructor on the conversion unit, having completed 18 missions over Iraq for *Southern Watch* operations. APM/BSS

The MBB Bo-105 CB3 09203/03 was a participant from the Swedish Army, based at No 25 anti-tank helicopter squadron with the OSTGOTA Army Aviation Battalion at Linköping, Sweden. The display pilot was Lt Hans Bergman, a 44 year old flight instructor – who gave his own commentary in English throughout his display. BSS

Hawker Hunter FGA9 XE601 made its first – and probably its last – flying display at an International Air Tattoo (although it has featured in the static line-up in previous years). Like the three Hunter T7s of the Boscombe Down fleet, XE601 is nearing the end of its working life and will shortly be replaced by a Jaguar. Sqn Ldr Dave Southwood AFC, a test pilot with DRA's Experimental Flying Squadron, regards the Hunter as 'his favourite aircraft' out of the 75 different types he has flown. DJM/GF

Every six years the BBMF's Lancaster undergoes major servicing and at this time receives a change of colour schemes and markings. 1994 coincided with such a change and PA474 embarked on the display scene wearing the markings of W4964 'WS-J' Johnnie Walker – an aircraft which operated with No 9 Sqn based at RAF Bardney, Lincs in 1944. Immediately, the most obvious change was the tail fins painted white on the outer sides. For IAT 94 the Lancaster was accompanied by Spitfire Vb AB910/AE-H and Hurricane IIc PZ865/J, but on this occasion the formation did not land at Fairford, having commitments at other events in the UK. DJM

1994 was the 30th year that the *Red Arrows* have represented the RAF. Initially the team was based at RAF Fairford in 1965, while being used as a satellite of the Central Flying School, its aircraft being HS Gnats. The team took delivery of BAe Hawk T1 jet trainers in late 1979, using the new aircraft in time for the 1980 summer display season. The new Team Leader for 1994 was Sqn Ldr John Rands, aged 34 – this being his second tour with the *Arrows*. At the start of the 1994 season the *Red Arrows* had performed no less than 2,805 public displays in 42 different countries – and will have added a further 100 performances by the end of this season. GF

CONCORDE'S 25th ANNIVERSARY

British Airways' Concorde G-BOAC made charter flights in and out of Fairford during the display period, on both days. This was specially arranged to mark its 25th Anniversary; as the British Concorde test programme was based at RAF Fairford from 1969 to 1977. G-BOAC was actually the first production Concorde built at Filton and arrived at Fairford in February 1974. On Saturday Concorde was flown by Capt Steve Wand and on Sunday by Capt Dave Rowland. PRM/APM/GF

On 23 August 1954 the first prototype of Lockheed's turboprop C-130 transport aircraft was airborne for the first time. Since that date over two thousand Hercules have seen service with military air arms and airlines right around the world. To mark this significant aviation milestone IAT 94 featured a 40th birthday party and gathering of C-130s.

It had been intended that there would have been a line-up of over 40 Hercules in an impressive display stretching the full length of Fairford's southern taxiway. Unfortunately this was not to be. Although 48 C-130s had notified their intentions of coming, a dozen of them called off during the week before the event. The crisis in Rwanda took away the L-100, Netherlands, French and other European Hercules, while the Haitian invasion stand-by kept a number of USAF C-130s on the far side of the Atlantic. Nevertheless, on the first day of the show 36 Hercules were in the line, thanks in no small way to last minute help from RAF Lyneham.

Featured prominently at the centre-point of the line were the four of the most notable C-130s. The very first production C-130A (53-3129) that had its maiden flight on 7 April 1955, was the first to be named Hercules and is now an AC-130A gunship; the 2,000th aircraft to be delivered – C-130H 91-1231 from the 165th Airlift Squadron, Kentucky Air National Guard; the distinctive ski-equipped LC-130H from the New York Air National Guard and Britain's Snoopy, the unique Hercules W2 with its long nose probe and high mounted radar operated for the Meteorological Office.

After their arrival on Wednesday 27 July there was a good deal of activity both on and off the airfield. Groundcrews busied themselves preparing their aircraft for the Concours d'Elegance competition – to find the best turned out aircraft. This was awarded to the LC-130H from the 139th Airlift Squadron NY ANG. A major C-130 symposium was held at Cheltenham, supported by Lockheed and other companies associated with the aircraft and its latest variant the C-130J.

A series of ground competitions were held at Fairford. The team from No 57 (R) Squadron, RAF Lyneham was judged to have carried out the best ground exercise by a UK crew, while the overseas award went to the Chilean Air Force crew from No 10 Group. Not surprisingly the Royal New Zealand Air Force crew from No 40 Squadron received the award for travelling the greatest distance to attend IAT 94 and they were also declared overall winners of the ground competition.

APM/PRM

ROYAL AIR FORCE

The RAF sent five aircraft from nearby Lyneham for the Hercules 40th anniversary line-up, comprising one of the five C1Ks (XV192), two C1s (XV292 and XV306) and two stretched C3s (XV202 and XV307). APM

MINISTRY OF DEFENCE (Procurement Executive)

The unique Hercules W2 *Snoopy* (XV208) is operated by the Meteorological Research Flight and used for weather reconnaissance and research tasks. Based at Farnborough for many years it is now with DRA at Boscombe Down. Unfortunately the future of *Snoopy* has recently been placed in doubt as a result of the withdrawal of funding by the Ministry of Defence as part of its continuing defence expenditure reductions. GF

ROYAL AUSTRALIAN AIR FORCE
C-130E Hercules (A97-160) – 37 Sqn

The RAAF operates two squadrons of Hercules under No 86 Wing from Richmond, New South Wales. No 36 Squadron has 12 C-130Hs and No 37 Sqn has 12 C-130Es. The Air Force is planning to replace its ageing C-130Es with the new C-130J. *APM/GF*

BELGIAN AIR FORCE
C-130H Hercules (CH-11) – 20 Sml/15 Wg

Belgium operates 12 C-130Hs in the Groupement de Transporto/No 15 Wing based at Brussels-Melsbroek. These C-130s are currently undergoing a major up-date and life extension programme. *APM*

BRAZILIAN AIR FORCE
C-130E Hercules (2458) – 1/1 GT

The Brazilian C-130E (2458 c/n 4061) is one of three used in the transport role with 1 Grupo de Transporte de Tropas, 2 Esquadrao, BA dos Afonsos at Rio de Janeiro. PRM

CANADIAN ARMED FORCES
CC-130H(T) Hercules (130341)
No 435(T) Sqn

Canada operates 30 C-130E/Hs in the transport, tanker and SAR roles with Nos 8, 14 and 18 Wings. This CC-130H(T) is one of five adapted as a tanker version and is based with No 435 (T) Squadron under No 18 Wing at Edmonton, Alberta. APM

CHILEAN AIR FORCE
C-130H Hercules (996)
Grupo 10

The Fuerza Aerea de Chile has a total of four Hercules for general transport duties. This C-130H 996 was from II Brigada/Ala 2, Grupo de Aviacion 10 at Merino Benitez AB, Santiago.
DJM/APM

ROYAL DANISH AIR FORCE
C-130H Hercules (B-678) – Esk 721

This C-130H is one of three of
the type operated by the Air Force with Tactical Air
Command (TACDEN), Eskadrille 721 at Vaerlose.
The squadron is also equipped with Gulfstream IIIs.
PRM

ITALIAN AIR FORCE
C-130H Hercules (MM61998) – 46 BA

The Italian Air Force forms part of
NATO's 5th Allied Tactical Air Force
and operates 12 C-130Hs in the
transport role. This C-130H (46-12)
is operated from Pisa-San Guisto by
50 Gruppo of 46 Aerobrigata. PRM

ROYAL JORDANIAN AIR FORCE
C-130H Hercules (347) – 3 Sqn

The RJAF operates four C-130Hs for transport duties. The veteran C-130Bs have recently been withdrawn from service owing to a shortage of spares. The C-130H, which had an extensive supporting exhibition with it in the static display was from No 3 Squadron at Amman-King Abdullah Airport. It was 'highly commended' in the Concours d'Elegance competition. DJM

ROYAL MALAYSIAN AIR FORCE
C-130H-30 Hercules (M30-10) – 14 Sqn

This was the first time that a Malaysian aircraft has appeared at IAT. The Tentara udara Diraja Malaysia operates six C-130H transports. This -30 stretched version is operated by No 14 Squadron from Kuala Lumpur (Subang) Airport. APM

ROYAL NEW ZEALAND AIR FORCE
C-130H Hercules (NZ7004) – 40 Sqn

The RNZAF Hercules made the longest flight to Fairford, taking six days by the Asiatic route. The crew was duly rewarded for its efforts with the appropriate prize. Five C-130Hs are operated by the RNZAF, all being operated by No 40 Squadron from Auckland-Whenuapi Airport. APM

ROYAL AIR FORCE OF OMAN
C-130H Hercules (503) – 16 Sqn

Three Hercules are operated as transports with the Royal Air Force of Oman. This light-sand camouflaged C-130H came from No 16 Squadron at Nassir Al-Qarni AB. DJM/APM

PORTUGUESE AIR FORCE
C-130H Hercules (16805) – 501 Esq

The Força Aérea Portuguesa operates four C-130Hs in the transport role and two stretched C-130H-30s for search and rescue duties. This aircraft (16805) is flown by Esquadra de Transporte 501, based at Montijo. PRM

SWEDISH AIR FORCE
C-130H/Tp84 Hercules (84004/844) – F7

The Svenska Flygvapnet operates two C-130Es (the first to be delivered to a European air arm) and six C-130Hs. The static Hercules, a C-130H (Tp84) was from Flygflottilj 7, Transportflygdivisconen at Satenäs. It carried impressive artwork on the port nose indicating it had undertaken 136 humanitarian missions into Sarajevo. BSS/APM

UNITED STATES AIR FORCE

The USAF sent a total of 15 C-130s to the 'Meet', ranging from the 39-year old AC-130A *'First Lady'* to the appropriately marked 2,000th aircraft, the C-130H *'Man O'War'* from the Kentucky ANG. There were nine different variants represented in the line-up, including an LC-130H and MC-130E. PRM/DJM

The AC-130A, first flown on 7 April 1955 as an original Roman-nosed C-130A (53-3129) suffered a major engine fire after landing at Marietta on its third flight a week later. It was rebuilt and flew again on 6 February 1956, subsequently being modified as a JC-130A for work on the Eastern Test Range and then as an AC-130A 'gunship' in the late 1960s for service in Vietnam. It received an armament array that comprised four GAU-2 7.62mm miniguns and four 20mm M-61s. After its service in SE Asia it passed to the Air Force Reserve, remaining as an AC-130A and is operated today by the 919th Special Operations Wing, 711th SOS, at Duke Field, Florida, with the appropriate name *First Lady*. APM/GF/PRM

Four standard C-130E transports featured in the anniversary line-up, coming from the 435th Airlift Wing/37th Airlift Squadron at Rhein Main AB, Germany (69-6566 *Boss Hog*); the 23rd Airlift Wing/2nd Airlift Squadron at Pope AFB, North Carolina (64-0539/FT); the 314th Airlift Wing/62nd Airlift Squadron at Little Rock AFB Arkansas (63-7778) and the Rhode Island Air National Guard/143rd Airlift Squadron (63-7788/RI), from Quonset Point State Airport, RI. The latter aircraft brought an OH-6A Cayuse from the 1-126th Avn Regt RI (Army) National Guard as an added feature for the static display. The smart 23rd AW aircraft from Pope AFB featured a shark's mouth marking on its nose and received special mention in the Concours d'Elegance competition.
PRM/GF

Of the two C-130Hs in the display line, 91-1231 was the 2000th Hercules off the production line, and had fin art work to this effect. On its nose it featured the markings *Man O'War* and *Thoroughbred Express*. It was from the 165th Airlift Squadron of the 123rd Airlift Wing Kentucky Air National Guard, based at Staniford Fd, Louisville. The second C-130H (84-0209) came from the Delaware Air National Guard, being operated by the 142nd Airlift Squadron of the 166th Air Group at Gtr Wilmington Airport, Delaware. GF/PRM/DJM

EC-130H 73-1590/DM featured the usual array of antenna and under-fuselage fins. The EC-130H is amongst the most distinctively modified members of the Hercules family and there are 16 aircraft in this category, which resulted from the *Compass Call* communications jamming project. Initial modifications were made to these C-130Hs in the early 1980s and there has since been a regular up-date programme. Although based in Germany for many years the 43rd Electronic Combat Squadron moved to the USA to join the 41st ECS at Davis Monthan AB, Arizona in 1992, where it remains under the control of the 355th Wing. APM

This HC-130H(N) (90-2103) is one of only three of the variant that were built for service with the Alaska ANG in the dual helicopter in-flight refuelling and rescue missions. They are broadly similar to the HC-130P, but incorporate state-of-the-art navigation and communications system. It is based with 210th Rescue Squadron of the 176th Composite Group at Kulis ANGB, Anchorage, Alaska. PRM

Three of the batch of 15 HC-130Ns originally produced for rescue-dedicated units of the Military Airlift Command were present at Fairford. They are based on the C-130H airframe and were configured to refuel Air Rescue Service helicopters in flight. They also have the AN/ARD-17 aerial tracking system in a hump over the cockpit. 69-5827 in green camouflage, was from the 352nd Special Operations Group/67th Special Operations Squadron based at RAF Alconbury. It carried three *Provide Comfort* mission symbols on its fuselage. 69-5832, in grey, was from the 16th Special Operations Wing/9th Special Operations Squadron at Eglin AFB, Florida. The second grey-painted HC-130N (69-5833/FL) came from the 301st Rescue Squadron AFRes based at Carswell AFB, Texas. APM/PRM/DJM

The HC-130P is also able to refuel helicopters in flight and entered service in late 1966 operations in South-East Asia, equipped with the upper fuselage AN/ARD-17 aerial tracker and the Fulton STAR personnel retrieval system. Hercules 64-14855/PD was built as an HC-130H and subsequently modified to HC-130P standard. It came from Portland IAP, Oregon where it is flown by the 304th Rescue Squadron. PRM

Four of the ski-equipped LC-130Hs were purchased in the mid-1980s for the New York Air National Guard as replacements for the original C-130D 'ski-birds'. Their primary mission is support of remote early warning sites in the Arctic. Provision for rocket-assisted take-off is incorporated in the LC-130H variant. 83-0490 *Pride of Clifton Park* came from 139th Airlift Squadron of the 109th Air Group at Schenectady County AP, New York. It was awarded the Hercules Concours d'Elegance trophy. PRM

Hercules 64-0561 is a *Rivet Clamp* version of the MC-130E, of which ten are currently in service. These have the 'chin' type of nose radome containing AN/APQ-122 and terrain following-radar and this example also has the Fulton recovery system. In addition, it possesses in-flight refuelling receptacles, an infra-red detection system, chaff and flare dispensers and radar warning gear. Finished in overall grey, 64-0561 came from 8th Special Operations Squadron of the 16th Special Operations Group based at Hurlburt Field, Florida. PRM/GF

**UNITED STATES
MARINE CORPS**

Marine Corps interest in obtaining a tanker version of the Hercules resulted in the acquisition of the KC-130F. Currently the Marine Corps has 67 KC-130 F/R/Ts on strength, but not all are permanently configured for tanker operations. Two tanks of 1,800 US gallons of fuel can be installed in the fuselage and transfer is effected via pod-mounted hose-and-drogue devices carried under each outer wing section. KC-130F Hercules 148249/GR-249, in light grey, was from VMGRT-253 based at Cherry Point, South Carolina. DJM

The stretched KC-130T-30 Hercules 164597/NY-597 is one of only two of the mark so far delivered to the US Marine Corps. The 'T' variant already had uprated engines, avionics and an inertial navigation system plus Omega and TACAN with the longer fuselage of the -30 giving even greater capacity. It is operated by the US Marine Corps Reserve tanker/transport unit VMGR-452 at Glenview, Illinois. GF

More than 30 air arms from around the world were represented in the static aircraft parks. These ranged from the Russian Navy's Tu-142 *Bear*, Swedish Air Force Lansen and French Air Force Mirage IVP to the Finnish Air Force Redigo, all making their IAT débuts this year.

ROYAL AIR FORCE

Bulldog T1 XX543/F, with its yellow and black rudder, is based with the Yorkshire University Air Squadron at RAF Finningley. GF

A regular participant in the static display at Fairford, No 6 FTS sent HS Dominie T1 XS713 from RAF Finningley. GB

A further representative from No 6 FTS at Finningley was this SA Jetstream T1 XX491 operated by No 45 (Reserve) Squadron, the RAF's Multi Engine Training Squadron. JD

From 735 Chipmunk T10s delivered to the RAF, this second production aircraft (WB550) remains in service with No 6 Air Experience Flight at RAF Benson. It is the oldest Chipmunk of the 66 survivors still flying with the RAF. PRM

Above: **Lockheed Tristar KC1 ZD950** from No 216 Squadron made the short flight across from RAF Brize Norton to be displayed in the 'Lockheed' line-up with F-16s in front and Hercules behind. DJM

Two Wessex HC2s were in the static display. The colourful **XT606** (right), with its red nose cowling and fuselage band, came from RAF Shawbury where it is operated by No 2 FTS. GF

One of three Nimrod MR2s that came to IAT 94, **XV254** was from No 201 Squadron at RAF Kinloss, having travelled a great deal further than VC10 C1K XV104 from RAF Brize Norton, that was displayed alongside it. PRM

Canberra T17A WJ633/EF from No 360 Squadron at RAF Wyton, made its final visit to IAT at Fairford this year. The ECM training squadron was due to disband in the following October and its Canberras retired. DJM

Left: SEPECAT Jaguar GR1A XX752 with the red *Flying Canopeners* markings of No 6 Squadron, flew in for static display from its base at RAF Coltishall. PRM

Below: One of the RAF Tornado GR1s that is based with the Tri-National Tornado Training Establishment at RAF Cottesmore, ZA352 coded B-04, was another welcome visitor this year. PRM

Only this single example of the Tornado F3, ZE209 from the F3 Operational Conversion Unit/No 56 (Reserve) Squadron at Coningsby, represented the RAF's principal front-line fighter aircraft. GF

Two Hawks from No 6 FTS were in the static display for the weekend, showing the changing colour schemes. Hawk T1A XX280 is finished in the standard grey colour scheme while T1 XX250 (left) has recently been repainted in the new standard gloss black scheme that all Hawks and Tucanos will eventually wear. DJM

The Strike Attack Operational Evaluation Unit sent grey-painted Harrier GR7 ZG475, one of four GR7s that it operates from A&AEE Boscombe Down. APM

ROYAL NAVY, ROYAL MARINES
& ARMY AIR CORPS

The Royal Navy contributed this Lynx HAS3 XZ730 to an impressive line of naval helicopters. It came from 702 Naval Air Squadron at Portland, Dorset – the unit that trains Lynx aircrew. APM

The Navy also provided two Westland Sea King helicopters. Still wearing its D-Day markings from earlier in the year, Sea King AEW2A XV664 (left) was flown in from RNAS Culdrose where it is operated by 849 Naval Air Squadron. The commando Sea King HC4 ZD480 did not have to travel so far, coming from 845 Naval Air Squadron at RNAS Yeovilton. GF

Also from the Somerset Naval Air Station was Westland Gazelle AH1 XX412 that is operated by 3 Commando Brigade Air Squadron, Royal Marines. APM

The Army Air Corps *Blue Eagles'* Westland Gazelle AH1 (ZA737) from 670 Squadron at Middle Wallop was positioned into the static display to be called upon during the weekend if necessary. APM

What was probably the final visit to IAT by a service Buccaneer, albeit a flight test aircraft from Boscombe Down, was made by 'raspberry ripple' painted S2B XW987. It is due to be retired, along with the other two remaining Buccaneers early in 1995. DJM

Above: **Canberras are now becoming a rare sight, both in the air and in static displays, therefore Canberra B2 (TT) WK128 was particularly welcome to IAT. It is flown as a target tug from the Test & Evaluation Establishment at T&EE Llanbedr.** APM

A pair of vintage Harvards are kept flying by the A&AEE at Boscombe Down, where they are used for air-to-air photography involving slower aircraft. They are also used for the training of pilots, where tailwheel practice is a requirement. Their arrival at Fairford was particularly noteworthy, being in formation with the Comet. APM

ASIA - PACIFIC TRAINING & SIMULATION PTE LTD

This is to certify that

R/D JAW R C MITCHELL

has attended

9/94 C-130 5-DAY REFRESHER COURSE
1 - 5 August 1994

conducted by

ASIA-PACIFIC TRAINING & SIMULATION PTE LTD
Training Centre, Singapore

5 August 1994

Date

Chief Instructor

ASIA - PACIFIC TRAINING & SIMULATION PTE LTD

This is to certify that

Raa'd Jaw R. C. Mitchel

has attended

2/95 C–130 5 DAYS REFRESHER COURSE

6 – 10 FEBRUARY 1995

conducted by

ASIA-PACIFIC TRAINING & SIMULATION PTE LTD
Training Centre, Singapore

_____
Chief Instructor

10 February 1995
Date

Above: **The ASTRA Hawk T1 XX341, has been specially modified as a variable stability aircraft for the ETPS. As the photo shows, it has recently received a replacement rudder that has not yet been painted.** APM

Left: **Just two Hunter T7s remain on active training duty with the RAF, both of which are operated by the ETPS and visited Fairford this year. XL564 was positioned in the static aircraft park and XL612 was parked on the north side of the airfield as a flying display back up for the FGA9.** PRM

Below: **Another of the 'raspberry ripple' painted ETPS aircraft in the static line-up was SEPECAT Jaguar T2 XX830.** PRM

BELGIAN AIR FORCE
(Force Aérienne Belge/Belgishe Luchtmacht)

Cleaning up on departure from Fairford are the two Belgian Air Force F-16A Fighting Falcons (FA-18 and FA-92) of 31 Smaldeel from 10 Wg Kleine Brogel. Belgium has just reorganised its F-16 squadrons, now having two combat wings with six squadrons. APM

CANADIAN ARMED FORCES
(Forces Armées Canadienne)

Canadian Armed Forces CP-140 Aurora of 415 Squadron, 14 Wing, of the Maritime Air Group, based at CFB Greenwood, Nova Scotia. The CP-140 combines the P-3 Orion airframe with the electronics of the S-3 Viking, and are exclusive to the Canadians. Auroras are located at two bases on the East Coast – Shearwater and Greenwood to cover the North Atlantic and one on the Pacific coast at Comox, British Columbia. DJM

CZECH AIR FORCE
(Ceske Vojenske Letectvo)

Once again the Czech Air Force has shown itself to be a stronger supporter of IAT and produced flying and static aircraft of types not always seen at western airshows. The Mil-17 *Hip* 0831(108M31) carried a 'Flying Hippo' badge on its door. This helicopter, fitted with a rescue hoist, is used for general transport, army support and rescue duties. DJM

Left: Once again the Sukhoi Su-25K *Frogfoot* 9013 (25508109013) of 30 BILP was displayed in the static park. This aircraft has become a regular visitor to IAT with its colourful depiction of the aircraft's NATO name, about to crush a tank with a hammer blow. PRM

This year the Czechs brought MiG-21s to Fairford for the first time. The aircraft in the static display was MiG-21MF *Fishbed* 7711 from the Flight Test Centre at Cáslav. It is painted in the markings of the 'Delta Acrobatic Group III' and was the spare for the flying display aircraft. PRM

ROYAL DANISH AIR FORCE
(Kongelige Danske Flyvevaaban)

A Gulfstream III of the joint Gulfstream/C-130 Eskadrille 721 departing for its base at Vaerløse. These twin jets are used for search and rescue, fishery protection and communications duties. PRM

Below: The tiny T-17 Saab Supporters (T408 and T415) of the Kongelge Danske Flyvevaaban have been regular visitors to UK airshows for many years. They are used at the Air Force Flying School and by squadrons and station flights as communications aircraft. APM

FORTY FIT FOR FIGHT

Below: *Forty fit for Fight* 40th anniversary markings were carried by F-16A E-191 (780191) of 730 Eskadrille Skrydstrup. Even the wing-tip Sidewinders had been painted up for the occasion. The Squadron badge (left) shows a more stylised bull in the form of 'Taurus'. APM

ROYAL DANISH NAVY & ARMY
(Søvaernets Flyvetjaeneste / Haerens Flyvetjaeneste)

Above: **Midnight blue painted Lynx Mk 80 S-170 is operated from shore bases and ships for fishery protection duties around the Faroes and Greenland. The Navy operates nine of these Lynx Mk 80s that are soon to be upgraded to Mk 90, with the fitting of Kestrel ESM tactical data systems and will receive uprated Rolls-Royce Gem 42 engines. Based at Vaerløse, the Lynx is maintained and operated under the joint 722 Esk.** APM

The Danish Army's Hughes Tow BGM-71 anti-tank missile armed SA550C-2 Fennec **(above). The smaller unarmed Hughes 500M (H201) (right) which accompanied the Fennec, is also used to support the Danish police when not needed for Army observation duties.** GF

FINNISH AIR FORCE
(Suomen Ilmavoimat)

A very welcome first-time visitor to IAT 94 was the Finnish Air Force Valmet Redigo RG-10 from the Finnish Flight Test Centre. The aircraft still under test is expected to be accepted by the Suomen Ilmaviomat as a basic trainer and for communications by the tactical wings. GF

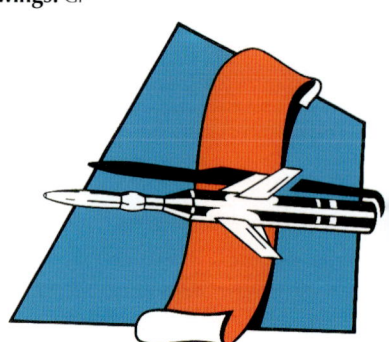

FRENCH AIR FORCE
(Armée de l'Air)

A French Air Force Mirage IVP is very rarely seen at airshows, even in France and this was the first visit of the type to a UK event. Flown by EB 1/91 from Mont-de-Marsan, Mirage IVP 55/CB is one of only 18 remaining in service, from the 62 originally built in the early 1960s. With a flat battery preventing its departure on the Monday after the show, the Mirage had to wait for a replacement to be flown in on the following day. PRM

FRENCH NAVY
(L'Aéronautique Navale)

The French Navy provided five different types of aircraft for the IAT 94 static display. Atlantique NG (17) from 24F at Lann Bihoué, is one of the new production models of the maritime patrol aircraft, that has been in service with the French Navy for many years. PRM

Sixteen SA321 Super Frelons are used for SAR and transport duties and No 162 attended from 32F at Lanvéoc. APM

FRENCH NAVY
(L'Aéronautique Navale)

The Falcon 10MER (129) came from ES57 at Landivisiau and is one of six in use for communications duties. PRM

Below: **The French Navy has 24 Lynx HAS2(FN)s in the ASW role and No 266 was from 34F, Lanvéoc.** DJM

Below: **EMB-121 Xingu (67) was from Lann Bihoué and is one of 25 used for training and VIP transport.** DJM

FRENCH ARMY AVIATION
(L'Aviation Legère de l'Armée de Terre)

The French Army Light Aviation sent three aircraft for the static display. AS332 M-1 Super Puma 2271/A1D that is used in the assault role, was from 4 Régiment d'helicoptères de Combat (RHC) with the Force d'Action Rapide at Nancy. DJM

Cessna F406 Caravan II 0010/AGT is one of a pair used for target towing/liaison duties operated by 3 GHL at Rennes. It was painted in the standard brown paint scheme with added dayglo red panels for higher visibility. PRM

GERMAN AIR FORCE & ARMY AVIATION
(Luftwaffe / Heeresflieger)

Four aircraft from the Luftwaffe appeared in the static display this year. The C-160D Transall (50+06), the oldest of the type still in service, was from LTG-63 at Hohn. It carried a very large colourful worker bee emblem on its freight door, as appears in the LTG63 badge. Transalls form the mainstay of the Luftwaffe's tactical transport fleet and are to be refurbished, to allow them to remain in service until 2010. APM

Representing the German Army was Sikorsky CH-53G 84+80 that flew in from HFlg Rgt 15 at Rheine-Bentlage. Three medium-transport helicopter regiments are equipped with 108 CH-53Gs and are concentrated in one army-aviation brigade, mainly supporting the combat troops. The CH-53s are currently undergoing a product-improvement programme to increase endurance as well as service life. PRM

GERMAN NAVY
(Marineflieger)

As usual IAT was well supported by the German Navy with an interesting selection of six different types of aircraft in the static display at Fairford. These included Atlantic 61+15, one of 19 in service with the Marineflieger, that flew in from MFG3 at Nordholz. This maritime-patrol aircraft has recently been modernised with new search radars, navigation systems and electronic-surveillance equipment. PRM

Dornier 28D-20U Skyservant 59+25 is a very distinctive aircraft and is one of only three remaining in service in Germany. This special mission Do28 is equipped with radar, FLIR and other sensors. It is operated on 'Freedom of the Skies' flights and for pollution monitoring by MFG-5 from Kiel-Holtenau. PRM

Sea King HAS41s are in the process of taking over the duties of the seven, blue painted former East German Mil Mi-8T *Hip* helicopters, that are being withdrawn from service. This helicopter (94+12) has been a regular visitor to UK airshows over the past three years. PRM

GERMAN NAVY
(Marineflieger)

Above: **The search and rescue Sea King HAS41 (89+55) was from MFG5 Headquarters at Kiel-Holtenau. The unit has detachments based at Borkum, Heligoland, Parow and Westerland.** PRM

This German Navy Lynx Mk 88 (83+10) (right), **known as a Sea Lynx, is shore-based with MFG3 at Nordholz, and is assigned to Type 122 frigates for anti-submarine duties.** APM

HUNGARIAN AIR FORCE
(Magyar Honvedseg Repulo Csaptai)

Antonov An-26 *Curl* (2209) made a return visit to Fairford this year. In 1993 it was parked on the north side of the airfield, this year it moved over to the static display. It is operated by the Szolnak Air Transport Regiment and brought in VIPs for the airshow. The Air Force operates more than a dozen *Curls* and *Cokes* in the transport role. APM

ITALIAN AIR FORCE
(Aeronautica Militaire Italiana)

The Italian Air Force supported IAT 94 extremely well, providing over an hour of the flying programme and eight aircraft in the static display.

The Italian AF Atlantic ASW force is undergoing a weapons system update programme and will subsequently incorporate the Iguane radar of the Atlantique ATL2. Atlantic MM40116/30-01, one of 18 on the Italian AF inventory, was from 30° Stormo/86 Gruppo at Galiari. It is the first of the up-graded Atlantics to be returned to service and can be identified by the new dorsal hump at the forward end of the fuselage spine. GF

A pair of Aermacchi MB339A MM54454/61-06 and MM54513/61-63 were amongst the last arrivals for the static display. They came from 61a Brigata Aerea at Lecce. DJM

Left: **Once again the Italian Air Force sent the ever-popular Starfighter to Fairford – in fact four examples, two single seat F-104S/ASAs and a pair of two-seat TF-104Gs. F-104S/ASAs MM6771/5-31 and MM6875/5-32 were from 5° Stormo at Rimini. They are employed in the attack role (although remaining examples are expected to be assigned to pure air-to-air duties in the near future). The TF-104Gs MM54258/4-40 (below) and MM54556/4-47 came from 4° Stormo/20 Gruppo at Grosseto.** DJM

ROYAL NETHERLANDS AIR FORCE & NAVY
(Koninklijke Luchtmacht / Marine Luchtvaartdienst)

The Royal Netherlands Air Force can always be relied upon to send a collection of F-16s to IAT. The four static examples were in the standard light grey colour scheme, devoid of any special markings other than fin top stripes and small squadron crests on their tails. The single seat F-16A(R) J-644 (right) carried a reconnaissance pod and came from 306 Sqn at Volkel; the three F-16Bs were: J-651 from 312 Sqn at Volkel, J-209 (below) from 322 Sqn at Leeuwarden and J-882 from 323 Sqn at Leeuwarden. These two airfields, together with Twenthe are now the main operating bases for the Dutch F-16s. PRM/APM

Below: **The Netherlands Navy has a total of 13 P-3C Orions of which most have now been brought up to P-3C update II standard, including the aircraft that visited Fairford (302). It was flown in from Valkenberg by a crew from 320 Squadron.** GF

74

RUSSIAN AIR FORCE
(Voenno-Vozdushniye Sily Rossioki Federatsii)

The Ilyushin Il-76MA *Candid* RA-78842 was the support aircraft for the Tu-95MS *Bear-H* from VVS Long Range Aviation (Dalnyaya Aviatsiya), that took part in the flying display on the second day. Although painted in Aeroflot colours and carrying a civil registration, the IL-76 was operated by VVS Transport Aviation (Voyenno-transportnaya Aviatsiya), flying in from Mozdok Air Base in the Northern Caucuses. The Russian Air Force is believed to have approximately 70 IL-76 transports and IL-78 *Midas* tankers in service, with most of the 76s painted in airline colours. GB/PRM

RUSSIAN NAVAL AVIATION
(Voenno-Mortskoy Flot Rossioki Federatsii)

This first Russian Naval Aviation aircraft to visit a western airshow, Tu-142M *Bear F* 93 (1603062) came from the Naval Training Regt in Southern Russia. Russian Naval Aviation has about 75 Tu-95/142M *Bears* on long-range maritime-reconnaissance and ASW duties. The Tu-142 *Bear F* is recognisable by its magnetic-anomaly detector (MAD) fairing at top of its fin. Production of the *Bear* has now ceased, 40 years after the first flight of the prototype. APM/GF

SLOVAK AIR FORCE
(Slovacke Vojenske Letectvo)

Recently Slovakia signed a bilateral defence treaty with Russia, which involved the supply of spares, hardware and training. Part of this package included some MiG-29A *Fulcrums* for the Air Force to bring the total up to 15 MiG-29As and two MiG-29UBs. One of the trainers, 1303 came from 1 SLP/1 Letka at Sliac Air Base for static display. This was finished in a special light grey colour-scheme with overall dark grey 'tiger' type stripes. PRM

A support Antonov An-26 *Curl* 2506 (12506) from 2ZDLP/2 Letka was also in the static display. This is the only An-26 *Curl* in the Slovak AF inventory. PRM

The RAF Benevolent Fund has received some surprise gifts in its 75 years – but one of the most unexpected presentations took place at IAT 94. When the pilot of the Slovak MiG-21 stepped out of the cockpit after touching down at Fairford he told officials "I won't be flying it back - its all yours!" In recognition of the assistance that the country's airmen received from the RAF Benevolent Fund, the Slovak AF presented MiG-21MF 7708 to the Benevolent Fund "with the intention of supporting its humane and noble mission in the year of its 75th anniversary". Prince Michael of Kent received the aircraft from Dr Pavol Kanis, Slovak Minister of Defence. The Fund was represented by Lord and Lady Barber and Air Chief Marshal Sir Roger Palin. PRM

MiG-21MF 7708 entered service with the CSAF's 6th Fighter/Bomber Regiment at Prerov on 7 July 1973, to replace obsolete MiG-15s. Following the split of Czechoslovakia, it was transferred on 30 October 1992 to the 81st Fighter Squadron at Sliac Air Base in Slovakia. It has flown a total of just over 1400 hours during its air force service. After IAT the MiG was flown to A&AEE Boscombe Down to be stored temporarily until it is auctioned for the benefit of the RAF Benevolent Fund. PRM

SPANISH NAVAL AVIATION
(Arma Aérea de l'Armada Espanola)

In the static was one of the Spanish Navy's three Cessna 550 Citation IIs, which are used for logistics/communications duties. U.20-1/01-405 was from Esa 004 based at Rota. APM

The Spanish Navy participated in the flying and static displays at IAT 94 for the first time this year, with a veteran AV-8S Matador in the static on Saturday, while awaiting replacement mainwheels from Yeovilton, alongside one of the Navy's two TAV-8S Matadors. This is the two-seat version used for training purposes. Although quite an old aircraft, VAE1-1/01-808 looked in immaculate condition, adorned with 'shark mouth' nose and black painted fin. APM

SWEDISH AIR FORCE & ARMY AIR CORPS
(Svenska Flygvapnet / Armeflygkar)

A Swedish Air Force Saab J-32 Lansen made its first UK airshow appearance at Fairford. Now a relatively old aircraft, the Air Force has only 23 J-32B/D/E versions remaining in service for target towing and ECM roles. The visiting aircraft 32512/03 was a J-32E version from F16M at Malmslatt (near Linköping). PRM/APM

Left: The Swedish Army has 20 MBB Bo105CBs in the anti-tank role, equipped with the Heli-TOW missile. Bo105CB/Hkp9B 09204/04, with a red marking on its tail boom, came from Armeflyget 2 at Malmstatt. GF

Right: The Swedish Air Force J-35J Draken 35607/07 was from F10 based at Angelholm near Malmo. A number of J-35Fs has recently been upgraded to J-35J standard to equip two Draken squadrons that will stay in service until the late 1990s, when they will eventually be replaced by the new JAS39 Gripen lightweight multi-role fighter. GF

UNITED STATES AIR FORCE

It was disappointing that no USAF aircraft took part in the flying display at IAT 94. However, the USAF did provide a wide variety of aircraft for the static line-up, as seen in this section with A-10s and F-15s much in evidence. Although no A-10 Thunderbolt IIs are now based in the UK, the type was represented by a pair of A-10As, 81-0952 and 81-0966 from the 52nd FW/81st FS at Spangdahlem, Germany. The USAF has now reduced its A-10/OA-10 inventory to 126 aircraft for the close-air support role – with only 20 remaining at the German base. Three versions of the F-15 Eagle were present in the line. F-15C 80-0035/IS and F-15D 81-0061/IS came from 35th Wg/57th FS at NAF Keflavik, Iceland. Two F-15E Strike Eagles, 90-0258/LN (with blue band on the tail) and 91-0313/LN (with red band on the tail) flew in from Lakenheath where they are operated by the 48th FW. GF/PRM

Two transports from the 86th Wing based at Ramstein AB in Germany – a C-9A Nightingale (71-0880) from the 75th ALS (right) and C-21A Learjet (84-0110) from the 76th ALS (above) made their regular visit to IAT. The USAF has a total of 23 C-9s and 72 C-21As in service . GF/DJM

UNITED STATES AIR FORCE

KC-10A Extender 83-0079, one of 59 of the type operated by the USAF, came from the 380th ARW/2nd AREFS at Plattsburgh AFB, NY. The overall grey-painted Extender was photographed during Saturday's display surrounded by parked cars and motor-cycles. PRM

Air Combat Command (ACC) sent a veteran B-52H Stratofortress and a relatively new B-1B Lancer for the static display again this year. The B-52H (below) was again parked next to its Russian contemporary – the Tu-142 *Bear*. B-1B 86-0132 (bottom), featuring the new overall grey colour scheme with large nose art, was from the 7th Wing, 337th BS at Dyess AFB, Texas. B-52H 60-0052 came from 5th BW/23rd BS at Minot AFB, North Dakota. PRM/GB

RC-135U 64-14847/OF based at Offutt AFB, NE with the 55th Wg/24th RS, the RC was on regular detachment to RAF Mildenhall, Suffolk where it is engaged in surveillance flights over the former Jugoslavia for the UN. PRM

Two KC-135R Stratotankers flew in to Fairford directly from the USA. 61-0272 came from the 434th Wg/72nd AREFS, AFRes at Grisson AFB, IN and 57-1469 from the 121st ARW/166th AREFS Ohio Air Guard at Rickenbacker ANGB, Ohio. APM

Below: **HH-60G Pavehawk 89-6206** made the 7-hour flight from Iceland where it is based with the 35th Wg/56th RQS at NAF Keflavik. It was refuelled in the air by an HC-130 Hercules during the long Atlantic journey to Scotland. PRM

Above: **Two USAF helicopters arrived for the IAT 94 static. Sikorsky MH-53J (69-5795)** had the relatively short journey to make from RAF Alconbury where it is operated by the 21st Special Operations Squadron of the 352nd Special Operations Group. It is one of 41 MH-53Js in service with the Special Operations Command, that has its headquarters at Hurlburt Field, Florida. GF

UNITED STATES ARMY

Above: **The US Army is the West's largest helicopter operator with more than 8,000 on strength, of which 3,300 are combat helicopters. One of the HQ European Command's Bell UH-1H Iroquois is a regular visitor to IAT. This year it was the smart brown and white painted 74-22514.** PRM

Left: **A clever arrangement brought a tiny US Army National Guard helicopter to IAT for the first time. Hughes OH-6A Cayuse 66-17792 from the 1-126th Avn, Rhode Island Army National Guard was airlifted in by compatriot C-130E (63-7788) that was attending the 40th anniversary Hercules meet from Quonset Point State Airport, RI.** DJM

Below: **The US Army also has some 450 fixed-wing aircraft, one of which, the twin-engined Beech RC-12K Huron 85-0147, with an array of aerials and fins, came from 1 MIB at Wiesbaden, Germany. The US Army operates 31 RC-12D/H/Ks in the ELINT role.** GF

UNITED STATES NAVY

Yet another regular participant in the IAT static display is the US Naval Air Facility at Mildenhall with one of its Beech UC-12Ms. The representative at IAT 94 was 163840/8G. DJM

The second US Navy representative was Lockheed P-3C Orion 159319/LA-5 from VP-5 *Mad Foxes* at NAS Jacksonville, FL. It was painted in the overall light grey with subdued markings and a stylised tail marking and code. PRM

CIVILIANS

Only a very small number of civilian aircraft, mainly former military aircraft, are invited to participate at an IAT event. This year there were just five present in the static display – a Basset, Sea Devon, Falcon 20 and Metro II.

Right: **Beagle B206 Basset CC1 XS770/G-HRHI** is finished in its former RAF Queens Flight colours. This was the Basset on which HRH Prince Charles undertook his twin-engine flight training. XS770 subsequently flew with the ETPS at Boscombe Down from 1975 to October 1986. It then went to the Aerospace Museum at RAF Cosford Museum, where it was put on display. It was purchased in 1989 by Cliff Basset who restored to flying condition again and now operates it from Cranfield. DJM

Left: **One of the two overseas based civil aircraft to be shown this year was the colourful Metro II PH-NLZ from the Netherlands NLR (National Lught En Ruimtevaartlaboratorium) in its distinctive orange, gold and green paint scheme.** PRM

Left: **Flight Refuelling has a big fleet of Dassault Falcon 20s based at Bournemouth International Airport to operate various military contracts. It includes five Falcon 20Cs, eight 20DCs, four 20Es and three 20Fs. Falcon 20DC G-FRAL was in the static park in its military training configartion.** PRM

Right: **DH104 Sea Devon C20 (a Dove 6)** was flown by the Fleet Air Arm as XK895 with the code 19/CU, signifying that it was based at *HMS Seahawk*/RNAS Culdrose. Although now in civilian ownership, having been registered as G-SDEV since March 1990, it retains its former RN colours, operating from North Weald. PRM

VISITORS

During the 'IAT 94 week' there was an appreciable number of visiting aircraft. Some were airliners or military transports bringing in passengers to watch the show, some brought in supporting groundcrew and others were simply practising and returning to their home bases. In the main VIPs arrived by helicopter, although a Royal Netherlands Air Force contingent arrived in style on board a B-25 Mitchell. After the event there were several visiting aircraft that brought in spare parts for 'sick' participants that had been unable to depart. The following is just a selection of this year's visitors.

Left: **Amongst the overseas charter flights were plain white and untitled Dash 8-301A PH-SDS of Schreiner Airways; Eurowings' ATR-42 D-BCRM; Saab 340B PH-KSA and Fokker 50 PH-KVF both of KLM/ Cityhopper.** PRM

Below: **When the Czech Air Force aircraft arrive at Fairford they fly over the airfield in a V-formation, headed by the supporting Tupolev Tu-134A. The transport aircraft brings in the groundcrews for the display aircraft together with spare parts and, at the same time, provides the navigation and radio contacts for the fighter aircraft. This year the lead aircraft was the Tu-134A *Crusty* 1407 from the 6th Air Transport Base at Prague-Kbely Air Force Base. The aircraft arrived on the Thursday, departed the same evening, and returned the following Monday to collect the personnel and aircraft for the flight back.** PRM

Above: **Two military transports, ETPS Andover C1 XS606 and Hercules C1 XV182 (Sat)/C3 XV189 (Sun) from Lyneham, operated to and from their home bases over the weekend with passengers.** DJM

King Hussein of Jordan made his usual visit to the show on Sunday, arriving in the Falcon of Friendship Sikorsky S-76B G-BTLA. Other members of his party arrived in Air Hanson Sikorsky S-76A G-BUXB. Both were parked together on the north side of the field. BSS

The North American B-25J Mitchell III (HD346/N320SQ) flew in from Rotterdam on the first day of the show. It is the flagship of a collection of vintage aircraft that is owned and flown by the Dutch group the 'Duke of Brabant Air Force'. It wears the markings of No 320 Sqn, a wartime RAF unit manned by Dutch airmen. PRM

An unusual Sunday visitor that parked on the north side was Roger Reeves' MH1521 Broussard G-BKPT that is attractively painted in a French Air Force desert colour scheme as No 192 '44-G1'. PRM

The Spanish Air Force support aircraft for the *Patrulla Aguila* was CN-235M T19B-20/35-28 from Ala35/352 Esc at Getafe. Finished in overall grey it looked as though it had just left the factory. It was parked alongside the Aviojets on the north side of the airfield throughout the weekend. APM

Two Let L-410s made short visits to Fairford. Supporting the Jordanian *Falcons* team was Bemoair's OK-WDJ on Wednesday 27 July and Monday 1 August. The Luftwaffe sent one of its four former East German Air Force L-410 UVP Turbolets (53+12) from the FBS at Cologne, arriving on Friday evening before the show with VIPs and departing 24-hours later. APM

EMERGENCY SERVICES

A show the size of IAT, with 165 static aircraft and eight hours of flying display requires an organisation which can respond effectively to ANY incident or emergency.

This year the fire teams were drawn from the Defence Fire Services (RAF, RN, Army), A&AEE Boscombe Down, British Aerospace at Dunsfold, AWRE Aldermaston, Birmingham International Airport, Chubb Fire Protection Ltd and the Fire Services College at Moreton-in-Marsh. There were also appliances from Gloucester County Brigade and the USAF at Fairford itself.

Similarly the medical services are drawn from members of the military and civilian organisations, including the Regular and Territorial Army Medical Services, the RAF and Auxiliary Air Force, USAF and Royal Navy Reserves. A Field Hospital of the RAMC (No 219) was located in a hangar on the airfield and was supported by elements of No 1 Air Evacuation Squadron, RAF. The civilian organisations came from the British Red Cross and St John Ambulance Brigade, the Gloucestershire Ambulance Service and numerous volunteers from Derbyshire, Cornwall, Mid-Glamorgan, Wiltshire, Somerset, Hampshire, Dorset, Berkshire, Surrey and the West Midlands.

There were three incident teams made up of IAT volunteers, members of the Field Regiment and the Royal Logistics Corps, Gloucester County Police and the RAF Provost Marshal. Further support agencies included the Women's Royal Voluntary Service and a team of chaplains.

Finally, and by no means least, there was helicopter support for the deployment of firemen, carriage of a fireball and the evacuation of casualties. These included Bolkow 105s of Bond Helicopters and Police Aviation Services, the latter also providing a Twin Squirrel; RAF Wessex HC2 from No 22 Squadron and two Royal Navy Sea Kings from 771 and 801 Naval Air Squadrons.

This large team, comprising nearly 500 personnel in total, worked together very effectively, having practised during the week of the show and conducted a full scale exercise for a simulated major disaster. Thankfully their services were not called upon other than for fairly minor incidents, the most noticeable of which was a taxying accident by the RAF Nimrod that struck a road-sweeper with its wing-tip.

Police Aviation Services Twin Squirrel getting airborne for traffic co-ordination, with the emergency response and evacuation Wessex and Sea King at readiness on the emergency services apron. BSS

This RAF Nimrod struck its wing-tip on a roadsweeper while taxying out for its flying display, the only airshow incident during the weekend. BSS

EMERGENCY SERVICES

Wessex HC2 of No 22 Squadron coming in to land for its emergency duty at IAT 94. BSS

Below: A full scale disaster exercise was held at Fairford on the Thursday before the show, to allow the different agencies to work together as a team. BSS

Above: RN Sea King HAR5 (XV661) of 771 NAS, Culdrose carrying a fireball to the crash scene during the exercise. BSS

THE RAF BENEVOLENT FUND'S INTERNATIONAL AIR TATTOO 94
PARTICIPATING AIRCRAFT

40th ANNIVERSARY HERCULES MEET

Royal Air Force

Hercules C1K	XV192	LTW
Hercules C1	XV292, XV306	LTW
Hercules C3	XV202, XV307	LTW

Ministry of Defence (Procurement Executive)

Hercules W2	XV208	DRA Met Research Flt

Royal Australian Air Force

C-130E Hercules	A97-160	37 Sqn

Belgian Air Force

C-130H Hercules	CH-11	20 Sml/15 Wg

Brazilian Air Force

C-130E Hercules	2458	1/1 GT

Canadian Armed Forces

CC-130H(T) Hercules	130341	435(T) Sqn

Chilean Air Force

C-130H Hercules	996	Grupo 10

Royal Danish Air Force

C-130H Hercules	B-678	Esk 721

Italian Air Force

C-130H Hercules	MM61998/46-12	46 BA

Royal Jordanian Air Force

C-130H Hercules	347	3 Sqn

Royal Malaysian Air Force

C-130H-30 Hercules	M30-10	14 Sqn

Royal New Zealand Air Force

C-130H Hercules	NZ7004	40 Sqn

Royal Air Force of Oman

C-130H Hercules	503	16 Sqn

Portuguese Air Force

C-130H Hercules	16805	501 Esq

Swedish Air Force

C-130H/Tp84 Hercules	84004/844	F7

United States Air Force

AC-130A Hercules	53-3129	711th SOS, AFRes
C-130E Hercules	69-6566	435th AW/37th ALS
	64-0539/FT	23rd Wg/2nd ALS
	63-7778/LK	314th AW/62nd ALS
	63-7788/RI	143rd ALS, RI ANG

C-130H Hercules	84-0209	142nd ALS, DE ANG
	91-1231	165th ALS, KY ANG
EC-130H Hercules	73-1590/DM	355th Wg/43rd ECS
HC-130H(N) Hercules	90-2103	210th RQS, AK ANG
HC-130N Hercules	69-5827	352nd SOG/67th SOS
	69-5832	16th SOW/9th SOS
	69-5833/FL	301st RQS, AFRes
HC-130P Hercules	64-14855/PD	304th RQS, AFRes
LC-130H Hercules	83-0490	139th ALS, NY ANG
MC-130E Hercules	64-0561	16th SOW/8th SOS

United States Marine Corps

KC-130F Hercules	148249/GR-249	VMGRT-253
KC-130T-30 Hercules	164597/NY-597	VMGR-452

AIRCRAFT IN THE STATIC DISPLAYS (SOUTH SIDE OF AIRFIELD)

Royal Air Force

Bulldog T1	XX709/12	CFS (YUAS loan)
	XX543/F	Yorkshire UAS
Canberra T17A	WJ633/EF	360 Sqn
Chipmunk T10	WB550/D	6 AEF
Dominie T1	XS713/C	6 FTS
Harrier GR7	ZG475	SAOEU
Hawk T1	XX228/CC	100 Sqn
	XX250	6 FTS/JFACSTU
	XX199	4 FTS/74(R) Sqn
Hawk T1A	XX280	6 FTS/JFACSTU
Hawk T1A (replica)	XX263	EP & TU
Jaguar GR1A	XX752/EQ	6 Sqn
Jaguar GR1A (replica)	XZ363/A	EP & TU
Jetstream T1	XX491/K	6 FTS/45(R) Sqn
Lightning F1A (nose)	XM191	EP & TU
Nimrod MR2P	XV254	201 Sqn
Tornado F3	ZE209/AV	F3 OCU/56(R) Sqn
Tornado GR1	ZD716/O	SAOEU
	ZA352/B-04	TTTE/C Sqn
Tristar KC1	ZD952	216 Sqn
Tucano T1	ZF487	1 FTS
	ZF344	3 FTS
VC10 C1K	XV104	10 Sqn
Wessex HC2	XT606/WL	2 FTS
	XR523/M	60 Sqn

Royal Navy

Lynx HAS3	XZ730/634	702 NAS
Sea King AEW2A	XV664/CU-180	849 NAS
Sea King HC4	ZD480/C	845 NAS

Royal Marines

Gazelle AH1	XX412/B	3 CBAS

Army Air Corps

Gazelle AH1	ZA737	670 Sqn *Blue Eagles*

IAT94 AIRCRAFT CHECKLIST

Ministry of Defence (Procurement Executive)

Buccaneer S2B	XW987	A&AEE/DGT&E
Canberra B2(TT)	WK128	DRA/T&EE Llanbedr
Harvard IIb	FT375	A&AEE/DGT&E
	KF183	A&AEE/DGT&E
Hawk T1 ASTRA	XX341	ETPS
Hunter T7	XL564	ETPS
Jaguar T2	XX830	ETPS

Belgian Air Force

F-16A Fighting Falcon	FA-18	31 Sml/10 Wg
	FA-92	31 Sml/10 Wg

Canadian Armed Forces

CP-140 Aurora	140103	415 Sqn

Czech Air Force

L-39MS *Albatros*	0005 (040005)	1 LSP/2 Letka
Mil Mi-17 *Hip*	0831 (108M31)	51 VRP
MiG-21MF *Fishbed*	7711	11 SLP
Sukhoi Su-22M-4 *Fitter*	4209/54 (42509)	20 SBOLP/32 ZTL
Sukhoi Su-25K *Frogfoot*	9013 (25508109013)	30 BILP

Royal Danish Air Force

F-16A Fighting Falcon	E-191	Esk 730
F-16B Fighting Falcon	ET-206	Esk 730
Gulfstream III	F-330	Esk 721
Sikorsky S-61A	U-278	Esk 722
T-17 Supporter	T-408	FLSK
	T-415	FLSK

Royal Danish Navy

Lynx Mk80	S-170	Esk 722

Royal Danish Army

Hughes 500M	H-201	Helikopterkompagni
SA550C-2 Fennec	P-234	P-HK

Finnish Air Force

L-90TP Redigo	RG-10	IlmaSK

French Air Force

Mirage IVP	55/CB	EB1/91

French Navy

Atlantique NG	17	24F
EMB121 Xingu	67	2S
Falcon 10 (MER)	129	57S
Lynx HAS2 (FN)	266	34F
Super Frelon	162	32F

French Army Light Aviation

AS532 Super Puma/ Cougar	2271/AID	4 RHC
Cessna F406 Caravan II	0010/AGT	3 GHL
SA342M Gazelle	4023/CYG	1 RHC

German Air Force

C-160D Transall	50+06	LTG-63
F-4F Phantom	37+01	JG-72
Tornado IDS	44+31	JbG-31
UH-1D Iroquois	71+64	LTG-63

German Army

Sikorsky CH-53G	84+80	HFR-15

German Navy

Atlantic	61+15	MFG-3
Do28D-20U Skyservant	59+25	MFG-5
Lynx Mk88	83+10	MFG-3
Mil Mi-8T Hal	94+12	MFHG
Sea King Mk41	89+55	MFG-5
Tornado IDS	45+28	MFG-2

Hungarian Air Force

Antonov An-26 *Curl*	209 (2209)	Szolnok Air Trans Regt

Italian Air Force

Atlantic	MM40116/30-01	30 Stormo/86 Gruppo
F-104S/ASA Starfighter	MM6771/5-31	5 Stormo/23 Gruppo
	MM6875/5-32	5 Stormo/23 Gruppo
Aermacchi MB339A	MM54454/61-06	61 Brigata/213 Gruppo
	MM54513/61-63	61 Brigata/213 Gruppo
TF-104G Starfighter	MM54258/4-40	4 Stormo/20 Gruppo
	MM54556/4-47	4 Stormo/20 Gruppo

Royal Netherlands Air Force

F-16A(R) Fighting Falcon	J-644	306 Sqn
F-16B Fighting Falcon	J-651	312 Sqn
	J-209	322 Sqn
	J-882	323 Sqn

Royal Netherlands Navy

P-3C Orion	302	320 Sqn

Russian Air Force

Ilyushin Il-76MA *Candid*	RA-78842 (03063)	Military Transport Aviation

Russian Naval Aviation

Tupolev Tu-142M *Bear-F*	93 bk (1603062)	Naval Training Regt

Slovak Air Force

Antonov An-26 *Curl*	2506 (12506)	2 ZDLP/2 Letka
MiG-21MF *Fishbed*	7708	1 SLP/2 Letka (Presented to the RAF Benevolent Fund)
MiG-29UB *Fulcrum*	1303 (N50903028113)	1 SLP/1 Letka

Spanish Navy

Cessna 550 Citation II	U20-1/01-405	Eslla 004
TAV-8S Matador	VAE1-1/01-808	Eslla 008

Swedish Air Force

J-32E Lansen	32512/03	F16M
J-35J Draken	35607/07	F10

IAT94 AIRCRAFT CHECKLIST

Swedish Army

MBB Bo105CB/Hkp9	09204/04	AF2

United States Air Force

A-10A Thunderbolt II	81-0952/SP	52nd FW/81st FS
	81-0966/SP	52nd FW/81st FS
B-1B Lancer	86-0132/DY	7th Wg/337th BS
B-52H Stratofortress	60-0052/MT	5th BW/23rd BS
C-9A Nightingale	71-0880	86th Wg/75th ALS
C-21A Learjet	84-0110	86th Wg/76th ALS
F-15C Eagle	80-0035/IS	35th Wg/57th FS
F-15D Eagle	81-0061/IS	35th Wg/57th FS
F-15E Strike Eagle	90-0258/LN	48th FW/492nd FS
	91-0313/LN	48th FW/494th FS
F-16C Fighting Falcon	91-0412/SP	52nd FW/23rd FS
	91-0415/SP	52nd FW/23rd FS
HH-60G Pavehawk	89-26206/IS	35th Wg/56th RQS
KC-10A Extender	83-0079	380th ARW/2nd AREFS
KC-135R Stratotanker	61-0272	434th Wg/72nd AREFS, AFRes
	57-1469	121st ARW/166th AREFS, OH ANG
MH-53J	69-5795	352nd SOG/21st SOS
RC-135U	64-14847/OF	55th Wg/24th RS

United States Army

Beech RC-12K	85-0147	1 MIB
OH-6A Cayuse	66-17792 (mkd as 0-17792)	1-126th Avn/RI ARNG
UH-1H Iroquois	74-22514 (mkd as 0-22514)	HQ USEUCOM

United States Navy

Beech UC-12M	163840/8G	NAF Mildenhall
P-3C Orion	159319/LA-5	VP-5

Civilian

Basset CC1	XS770 (G-HRHI)	City Air Charter
Cessna 340A	HB-LPK	Bruno Stocker
DH Sea Devon C20	XK895/CU-19 (G-SDEV)	Peter Gill & W.Gentle
Falcon 20DC	G-FRAL	FR Aviation
Metro II	PH-NLZ	NLR

AIRCRAFT IN THE FLYING DISPLAY (AND SPARES) ON FLIGHTLINES (NORTH SIDE)

Royal Air Force

Harrier GR7	ZD435/04	1 Sqn
	ZD378/A	HOCU/20(R) Sqn
Hawk T1	XX231	7 FTS/19(R) Sqn
	XX178/M	7 FTS/92(R) Sqn
Hercules C1	XV185	LTW
	XV218	LTW
Jaguar GR1A	XX116	16(R) Sqn
Nimrod MR2P	XV239	201 Sqn
	XV246 (Sun only)	201 Sqn
Tornado GR1	ZA559/F	15(R) Sqn
	ZA607/TJ	15(R) Sqn
Tucano T1	ZF408	1 FTS
	ZF514	1 FTS
Wessex HC2	XT602	22 Sqn/SARTU

Royal Navy

Gazelle HT2	XX441/CU-38	705 NAS
	XZ942/CU-42	705 NAS
Sea King HAR5	XV661/CU-824	771 NAS
Sea King HAS6	ZA129/CU-502	810 NAS

Army Air Corps

Gazelle AH1	XW897	670 Sqn *Blue Eagles*
	XZ310	670 Sqn *Blue Eagles*
	XZ344	670 Sqn *Blue Eagles*
	ZB666	670 Sqn *Blue Eagles*
Lynx AH7	XZ675/E	671 Sqn *Blue Eagles*

Ministry of Defence (Procurement Executive)

Comet 4C	XS235	A&AEE/DGT&E
Hunter FGA9	XE601	A&AEE/DGT&E
Hunter T7	XL612	ETPS

Belgian Air Force

F-16A Fighting Falcon	FA-107	1 Sml/2 Wing
	FA-112	2 Sml/2 Wing

Czech Air Force

Antonov An-26 *Curl*	2409 (12409)	3 DVLP
L-39MS *Albatros*	0004/62 (040004)	1 LSP/2 Letka
LET L-410UVP *Turbolet*	0926/4 (820926)	1 DVLP/6 ZDL *Szobi Kvartet*
	0928/1 (820928)	1 DVLP/6 ZDL *Szobi Kvartet*
	0929/2 (820929)	1 DVLP/6 ZDL *Szobi Kvartet*
	1132/3 (831132)	1 DVLP/6 ZDL *Szobi Kvartet*
MiG-21MF *Fishbed*	4307	11 SLP
Mil Mi-24D *Hind*	0216 (M340216)	51 VRP
	4011 (M344011)	51 VRP
Sukhoi Su-22M-4 *Fitter*	4006/31 (40306)	20 SBOLP/32 zTL
Sukhoi Su-25K *Frogfoot*	1002 (25508110002)	30 BILP

French Air Force

Alpha Jet E (Thursday and Sunday only)	E23/1 (F-TERO)	*Patrouille de France*
	E121/2 (F-TERK)	*Patrouille de France*
	E125/3 (F-TERH)	*Patrouille de France*
	E89/4 (F-TERE)	*Patrouille de France*
	E132/5 (F-TERN)	*Patrouille de France*
	E140/6 (F-TERD)	*Patrouille de France*
	E121/7 (F-TERK)	*Patrouille de France*
	E106/8 (F-TERJ)	*Patrouille de France*
	E72/9 (F-TERG)	*Patrouille de France*
	E97/0 (F-TERL)	*Patrouille de France*
C-160NG Transall	F207/64-GG	ET2/64
Mirage 2000B	516/2-FM	EC2/2
	521/2-FX	EC2/2

German Air Force

F-4F Phantom	37+36	JG-73
	37+06	JG-73
Tornado IDS	44+68	JbG-32
Tornado ECR	46+34	JbG-32

German Navy

Tornado IDS	46+14	MFG-2

Italian Air Force

Aermacchi MB339PAN	MM54439/6	*Frecce Tricolori*
	MM54473/4	*Frecce Tricolori*
	MM54477/9	*Frecce Tricolori*
	MM54478/7	*Frecce Tricolori*
	MM54479/1	*Frecce Tricolori*
	MM54480/0	*Frecce Tricolori*
	MM54482/5	*Frecce Tricolori*
	MM54483/13	*Frecce Tricolori*
	MM54484/3	*Frecce Tricolori*
	MM54485/10	*Frecce Tricolori*
	MM54486/2	*Frecce Tricolori*
Aeritalia G222	MM62130/RS-51	RSV/311 Gruppo
AMX Centaur	MM7149/51-53	51 Stormo
	MM7131/RS-13/52	RSV/311 Gruppo
Piaggio P180 Avanti	MM62164	RSV/311 Gruppo

Royal Netherlands Air Force

Alouette III	A-324	*Grasshoppers*
	A-350	*Grasshoppers*
	A-398	*Grasshoppers*
	A-453	*Grasshoppers*
	A-465	*Grasshoppers*
F-16A Fighting Falcon	J-251	313 Sqn
	J-256	313 Sqn

Royal Netherlands Navy

SH-14D Lynx	272	860 Sqn

Russian Air Force

Tupolev Tu-95MS *Bear-H*	23 bk (34379)	182nd Heavy Bomber Sqn

Slovak Air Force

MiG-21MF *Fishbed*	7714	3 SBOLP
MiG-29A *Fulcrum*	9308 (26393)	1 SLP/1 Letka
L-39C Albatros	0101 (530101)	*White Albatros*
	0102 (530102)	*White Albatros*
	0111 (530111)	*White Albatros*
	0112 (530112)	*White Albatros*
	0443 (430443)	*White Albatros*
	4355 (834355)	*White Albatros*
	4357 (834357)	*White Albatros*

Spanish Air Force

CASA C101ED Aviojet	E25-06/79-06/6	*Patrulla Aguila*
	E25-07/79-07/7	*Patrulla Aguila*
	E25-08/79-08/8	*Patrulla Aguila*
	E25-13/79-13/3	*Patrulla Aguila*
	E25-22/79-22/13	*Patrulla Aguila*
	E25-25/79-25/5	*Patrulla Aguila*
	E25-27/79-27/11	*Patrulla Aguila*
	E25-28/79-28/12	*Patrulla Aguila*
CASA/IPTN CN235	T19B-20/35-28	Ala 35/352 Esc

Spanish Navy

AV-8S Matador	VA1-3/01-804	Escuadrilla 008

Swedish Air Force

C-130E/Tp84 Hercules	84001/841	F7
J-35F Draken	35520/14	F10
	35531/31	F10

Swedish Army

MBB Bo105CB/Hkp9	09203/03	AF2

Swiss Air Force

Hunter F58	J-4020	*Patrouille Suisse*
	J-4021	*Patrouille Suisse*
	J-4022	*Patrouille Suisse*
	J-4025	*Patrouille Suisse*
	J-4029	*Patrouille Suisse*
	J-4030	*Patrouille Suisse*
	J-4031	*Patrouille Suisse*

Civilian

DH115 Vampire T55	G-BVLM	RV Aviation/RJAF Hist Flt
Extra 300	JY-RNA (036)	*Royal Jordanian Falcons*
	JY-RNC (038)	*Royal Jordanian Falcons*
	JY-RND (039)	*Royal Jordanian Falcons*
	JY-RNE (042)	*Royal Jordanian Falcons*
MBB Bo105DBS/4	G-BUXS	Bond Helicopters Ltd
	G-PASG	Police Aviation Services
Spitfire LFIX	MK732/OU-U (G-HVDM)	Dutch Spitfire Flt

FLYING DISPLAY AIRCRAFT (DID NOT LAND) SATURDAY 30 JULY AND SUNDAY 31 JULY

Stearman A75	N54922	*Crunchie Flying Circus*
	G-IIIG	*Crunchie Flying Circus*
Super Stearman	N5057V	*Crunchie Flying Circus*
Sea King HAR3	XZ588	RAF SKTU (Sat only)
Hercules C1	XV179	RAF LTW
	XV293	RAF LTW
Hercules C1K	XV201	RAF LTW (Sat only)
Hercules C3	XV212	RAF LTW (Sun only)
	XV294	RAF LTW (Sat only)
	XV303	RAF LTW
Tristar C2	ZE704	RAF 216 Sqn
VC10 C1K	XV101	RAF 10 Sqn
VC10 K3	ZA149	RAF 101 Sqn
Lancaster B1	PA474/WS-J	RAF BBMF
Hurricane IIc	PZ865/J	RAF BBMF
Spitfire Vb	AB910/AE-H	RAF BBMF
Hawk T1	XX233	RAF *Red Arrows*
	XX237	RAF *Red Arrows*
	XX294	RAF *Red Arrows*
Hawk T1A	XX227	RAF *Red Arrows*
	XX252	RAF Red Arrows
	XX253	RAF Red Arrows
	XX260	RAF Red Arrows
	XX264	RAF Red Arrows
	XX266	RAF Red Arrows

IAT94 AIRCRAFT CHECKLIST

VISITING, SUPPORT AND CHARTER AIRCRAFT
BETWEEN 27 JULY – 1 AUGUST

Wednesday 27 July

Hawk T1	XV219	RAF 7FTS/19(R) Sqn
Hercules C1	XV295	RAF LTW
	XV206	RAF LTW
	XV218	RAF LTW
Hercules C3	XV212	RAF LTW
LET L-410UVP Turbolet	OK-WDJ	Bemoair

Thursday 28 July

Comet 4C	XS235	A&AEE/DGT & E
DH115 Vampire T55	G-BVLM	RV Aviation/RJAF Hist Flt
Gazelle HCC4	XW852	RAF 32 Sqn
Hercules C1	XV181	RAF LTW
	XV295	RAF LTW
	XV205	RAF LTW
	XV206	RAF LTW
Hercules C1K	XV203	RAF LTW
Hercules C3	XV176	RAF LTW
	XV217	RAF LTW
Hunter T7	800/F (G-BOOM)	RV Aviation/RJAF Hist Flt
Learjet 35A	T-781	Swiss AF VIP Flight
	T-782	Swiss AF SF Dubendorf
Merlin IIIA	CF-01	Belgian AF 21 Sml
Mil Mi-8T *Hip*	94+08	German Navy MFHG
PA-23 Aztec 250E	G-BATN	Marshall Aerospace
Tornado F3	ZE737/FF	RAF 25 Sqn
	ZE162/FK	RAF 25 Sqn
Tupolev Tu-134A *Crusty*	1407 (320805)	Czech AF 6 ZDLP, Kbely

Friday 29 July

Andover C1	XS606	MoD(PE) ETPS
AS 355F-1 Twin Squirrel	G-PASE	Police Aviation Servs
Chipmunk T10	WB586/A	RAF 6 AEF
Citation 550	G-BFRM	Marshall Engineering
Dominie T1	XS726/T	RAF 6 FTS
F27M-100 Friendship	C-2	R Netherlands AF 334 Sqn
Falcon 20F	G-FRAA	FR Aviation
LET L-410UVP Turbolet	53+12 (800527)	German AF FBS-BMvg
Tornado IDS	45+45	German Navy MFG-2
Tristar KC1	ZD952	RAF 216 Sqn
VC10 C1K	XV109	RAF 10 Sqn
VC10 K4	ZD240	RAF 101 Sqn

Saturday 30 July

Andover C1	XS606	MoD(PE) ETPS
ATR-42	D-BCRM	Eurowings
AS 355F-1 Twin Squirrel	G-ZFDB	Lynton Aviation
BAe 125 CC3	ZD620	RAF 32 Sqn
B-25J Mitchell	HD346/NO-V (N320SQ)	Duke of Brabant AF
Bell 206B JetRanger II	G-UEST	CSE
Concorde	G-BOAC	British Airways
Douglas DC-3	G-AMPZ	Air Atlantique
	G-AMRA	Air Atlantique

Dash 8-301 … (continued)

Dash 8-301	PH-SDS	Schreiner Airways
Falcon 20F	G-FRAA	FR Aviation
Fokker 50	PH-KVF	KLM CityHopper
Gazelle HCC4	XW852	RAF 32 Sqn
Gazelle HT3	ZA804/I	RAF 2 FTS
Hercules C1	XV182	RAF LTW
Learjet 35A	T-782	Swiss AF SF Dubendorf
SAAB 340B	PH-KSC	KLM CityHopper

Sunday 31 July

Andover C1	XS606	MoD(PE) ETPS
BAe 125 CC3	ZE395	RAF 32 Sqn
Bell 206A Jet Ranger 2	G-ONOW	Mega Yield Ltd
Bell 206B Jet Ranger 2	G-STOX	Burman Helicopters
Concorde	G-BOAC	British Airways
DC-3 Dakota	PH-DDA	Dutch Dakota Assoc
	G-AMPZ	Air Atlantique
	G-AMRA	Air Atlantique
Dash 8-301	PH-SDS	Schreiner Airways
F27-100 Friendship	PH-KFG	F-27 Friendship Assoc
Falcon 20F	G-FRAA	FR Aviation
Gazelle HT3	ZA804/I	RAF 2 FTS
Gazelle HCC4	XW852	RAF 32 Sqn
Hercules C1	XV189	RAF LTW
MH1521M Broussard	192/44-GI (G-BKPT)	Roger Reeves
SAAB 340B	PH-KSC	KLM CityHopper
Sikorsky S-76A	G-BUXB	Air Hanson
Sikorsky S-76B	G-BTLA	Falcon of Friendship

Monday 1 August

Andover C1	XS606	MoD(PE) ETPS
B200 King Air	HB-GDL	FOCA
Learjet 35A	T-782	Swiss AF SF Dubendorf
Mystere 20	F-UKJA	French AF CIFAS-328
Tupolev Tu-134A *Crusty*	1407	Czech AF 6 ZDLP, Kbely

Tuesday 2 August

Aeritalia G222	MM62104	Italian AF
Aerospatiale TBM-700	70/43-XC	French AF EL-43
BAe 125 CC3	ZD620	RAF 32 Sqn
F-16B Fighting Falcon	J-651	R Neth AF 312 Sqn

Wednesday 3 August

F-27 Troopship	C-12	R Neth AF 334 Sqn
HS Nimrod MR2	XV240	RAF 120 Sqn

Thursday 4 August

F-16B Fighting Falcon	J-068	R Neth AF 313 Sqn
Sikorsky S-61A	U-278	R Danish AF Esk 722

Last departures

AC-130A Hercules	53-3129	To USA on Friday 5 August
Tornado IDS	46+14	To Germany on Thursday 18 August

RAF BENEVOLENT FUND ENTERPRISES PUBLICATIONS

Titles available in this series:

01. INTERNATIONAL AIR TATTOO 93
The world's largest military air show
Published October 1993
ISBN 0-9516581-4-X
Price £10.95

02. MIGHTY HERCULES
The first four decades
Published July 1994
ISBN 0-9516581-6-6
Price £14.95

03. INTERNATIONAL AIR TATTOO 94
The best in military aviation
Published October 1994
ISBN 0-9516581-7-4
Price £10.95

04. ROYAL AIR FORCE ALMANAC 1995
A directory of the RAF
Published October 1994
ISBN 0-9516581-8-2
Price £14.95

For postage on the above titles add £1.50 UK; £2.50 Europe; £3 Outside Europe
by Surface Mail for each publication.

* Also available the special edition
BRACE BY WIRE TO FLY-BY-WIRE
Celebrating the 75th Anniversary of the Royal Air Force Benevolent Fund
This magnificent book is a tribute to the 75 year history of both the Fund and the Royal Air Force.
Fine colour prints by leading aviation artists depict individual years of RAF service, each faced by
informative text appropriate to that year.
ISBN 0-9516581-3-1 Hardback – 168pp, sturdy slipcase
Price: £34.95 inc p&p (UK); £36.95 inc p&p (overseas).

These books are available from RAF Benevolent Fund Enterprises Publishing, Building 15, RAF Fairford,
Glos GL7 4DL, England. Send IMO or Sterling cheque drawn on UK Bank payable to RAFBF Enterprises or
charge made against Visa or Access/Mastercard – please quote Card No, name of bearer and expiry date.
Tel: 0285 713300 Fax: 0285 713268.